The Color of Loss

The Color of Loss

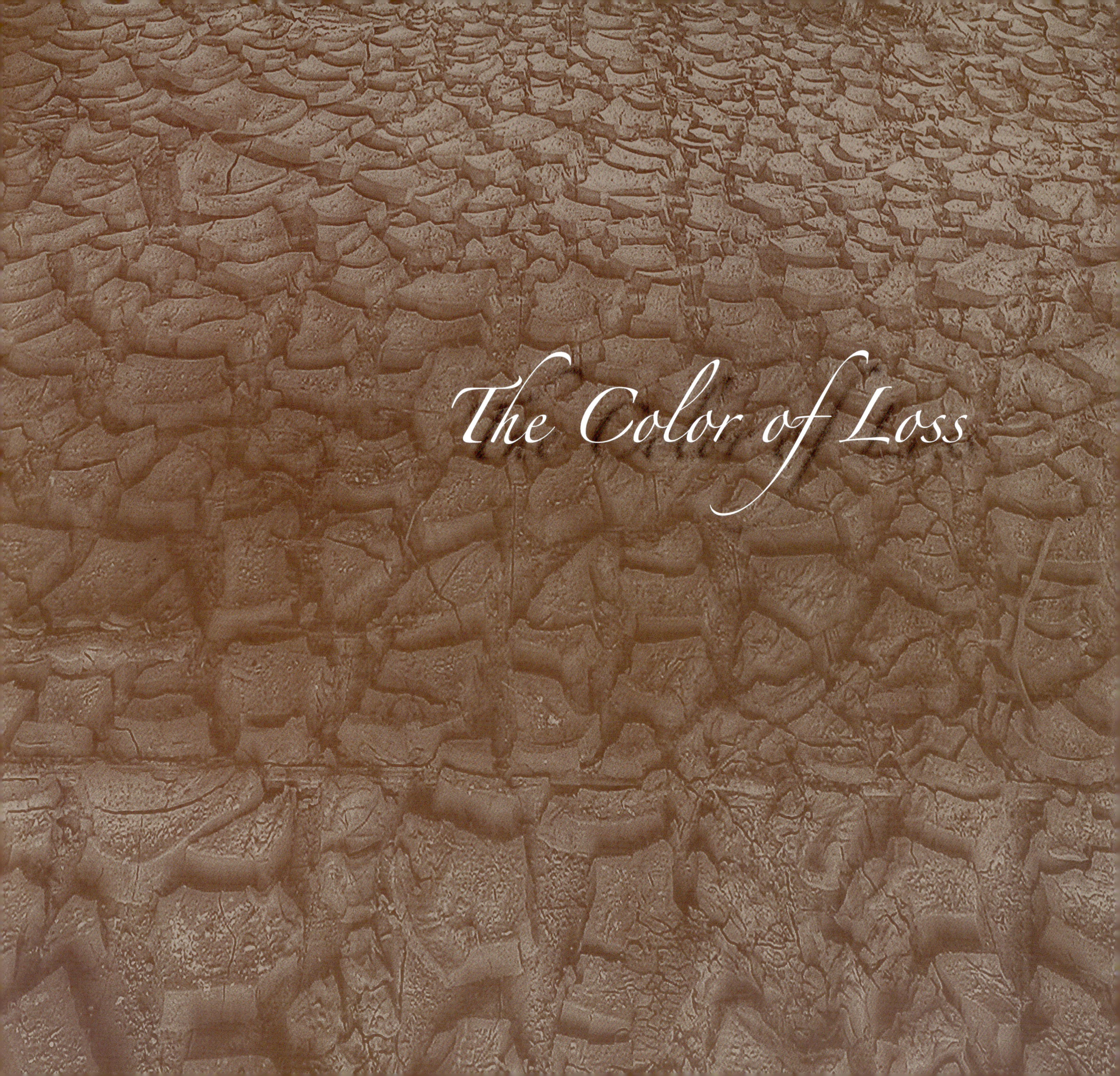

AN INTIMATE PORTRAIT OF NEW ORLEANS AFTER KATRINA

Photographs and Introduction by
DAN BURKHOLDER

Foreword by
ANDREI CODRESCU

University of Texas Press *Austin*

The publication of this book was made possible by a generous contribution from the University of Texas Press Advisory Council.

Printed in China
First edition, 2008

∞ The paper used in this book meets the minimum requirements of ANSI/NISO Z39.48-1992 (R1997) (Permanence of Paper).

LIBRARY OF CONGRESS
CATALOGING-IN-PUBLICATION DATA

Burkholder, Dan, 1950–
The color of loss : an intimate portrait of New Orleans after Katrina / photographs and introduction by Dan Burkholder ; foreword by Andrei Codrescu. — 1st ed.
p. cm.
ISBN 978-0-292-71713-8 (cloth : alk. paper)
1. New Orleans (La.) — Pictorial works. 2. Hurricane Katrina, 2005 — Pictorial works. 3. Hurricane damage — Louisiana — New Orleans — Pictorial works. 4. New Orleans (La.) — Buildings, structures, etc. — Pictorial works. 5. Abandoned buildings — Louisiana — New Orleans — Pictorial works. 6. House furnishings — Louisiana — New Orleans — Pictorial works. 7. Personal belongings — Louisiana — New Orleans — Pictorial works. 8. Interior architecture — Louisiana — New Orleans — Pictorial works. 9. Photography, Artistic. 10. Photography — Digital techniques. I. Title.
F379.N543B87 2008
976.3'350640222—dc22

2007033009

To the people of New Orleans,
whose generosity, kindness, creativity,
and spirit will survive any storm or
government failure.

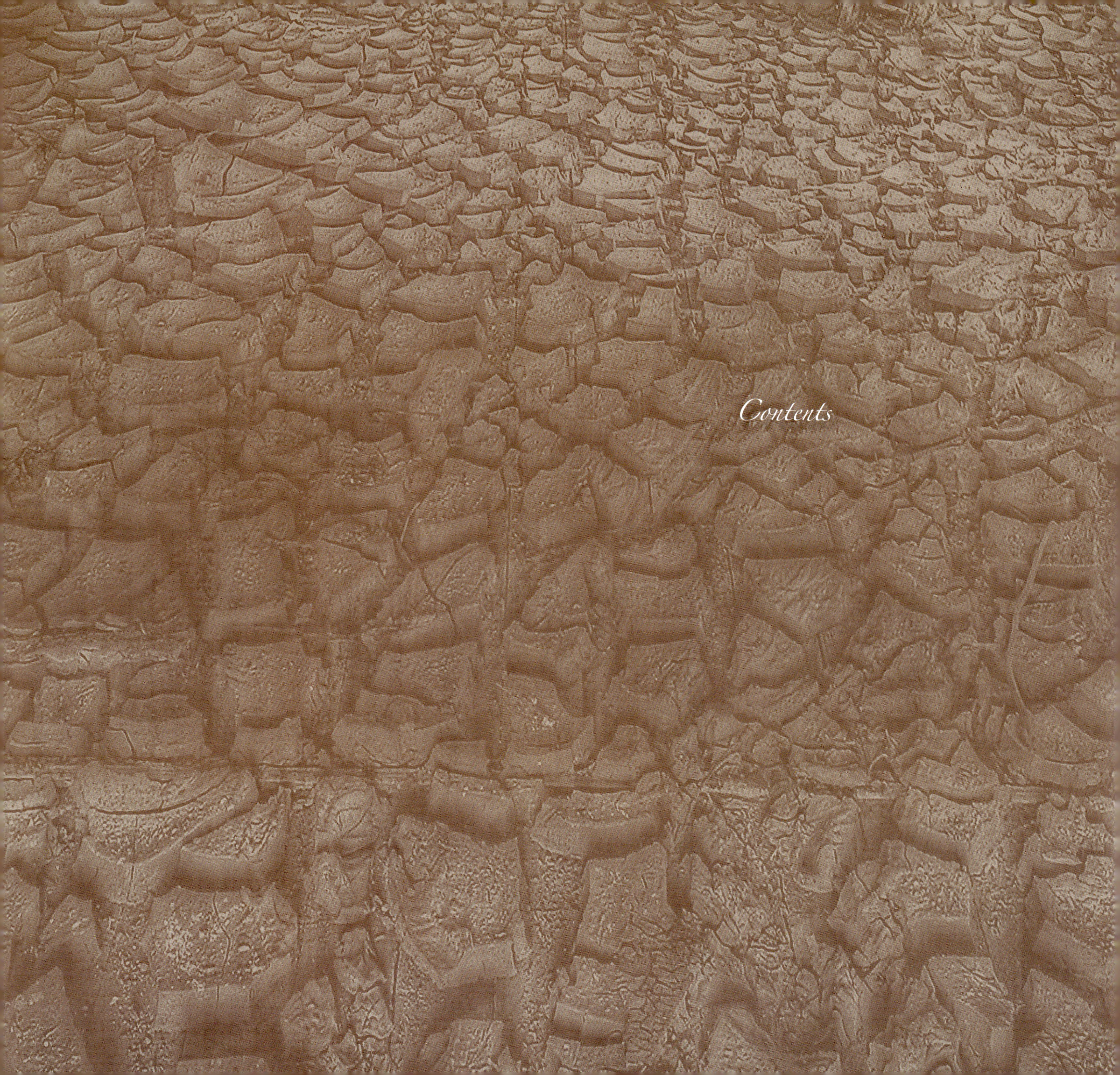

Contents

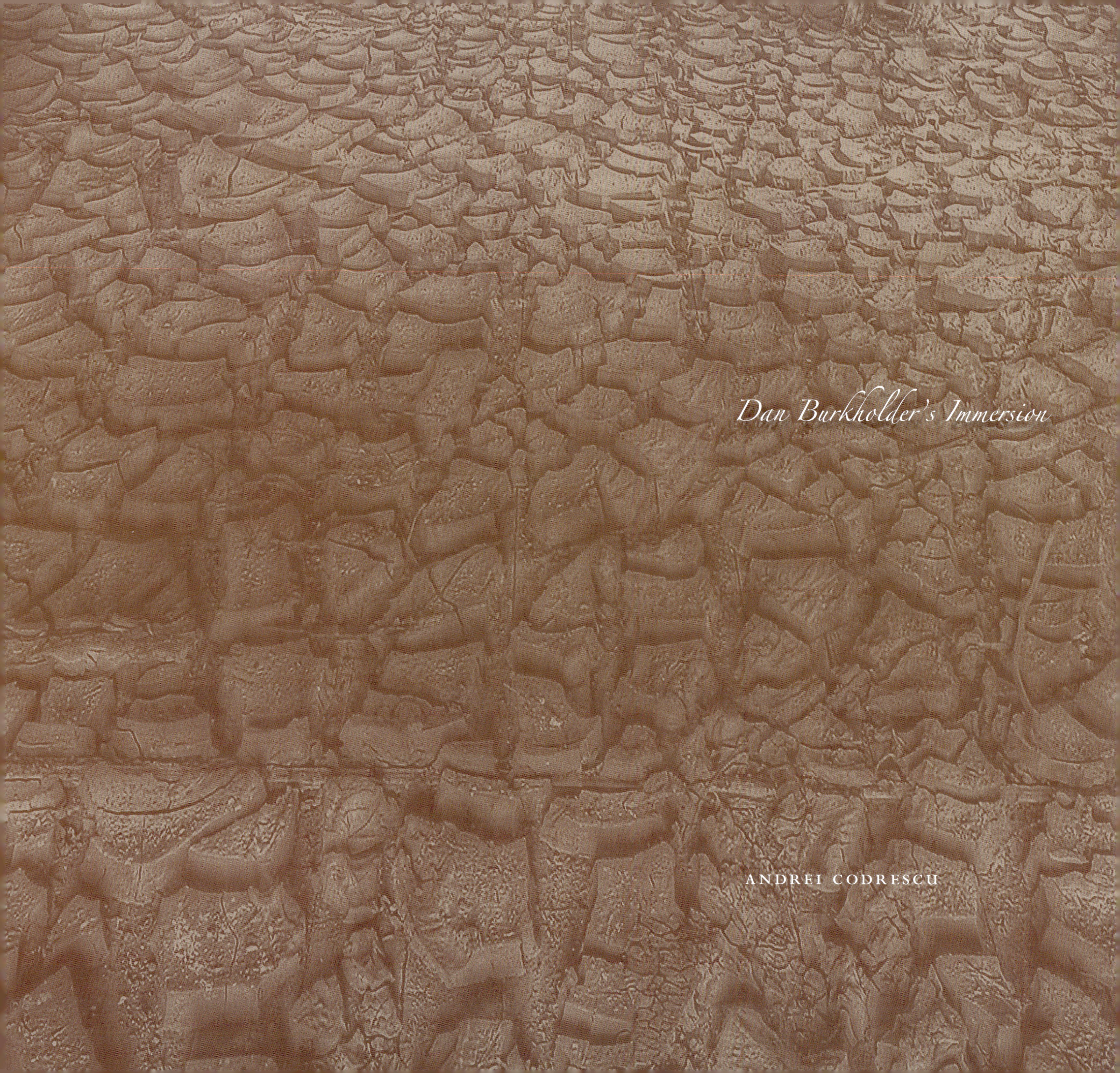

Dan Burkholder's Immersion

ANDREI CODRESCU

On the simplest level, Dan Burkholder has photographed the everyday objects inside homes destroyed by the Catastrophe known as Katrina. But like the Catastrophe, the name Katrina is only a cover for multiple realities, only one of which is the hurricane by that name. Others include the breaching of the levees after the Storm, the greatest engineering failure in American history; the complete emptying of the city by the departure of its inhabitants; the unreal heat and stillness that descended on the drowned and emptied city after the winds died down; and the rise from the fetid water of hellish molds that began to hungrily devour what the wind and the first floods had spared. Outside the houses into which Burkholder went to point his camera, there was a sun-broiled hell over a lake in which floated much of what was inside people's homes and, quite often, the bodies of the people and pets who had inhabited some of those homes. We saw this outside hell because the television cameras were there almost instantly. We received this New Orleans in our living rooms via TV and radio, and we saw and heard the cries for help from people crowded in nightmarish conditions in the Superdome and the Civic Center. It turned out that many people, including a great number of the old and sick, had not evacuated the city. But they did evacuate their homes, which stood drowning in water, eaten by molds even as rescues and news coverage went on outside.

Inside those empty homes, the molds went to work, ghoulish creatures with faces and personalities, living demons with huge appetites. The only humans who entered the flooded homes after the waters drew back were inspectors looking for bodies and, occasionally, thieves. These interiors were unhealthy places. In addition to the molds, there were toxic releases from ripped insulation, exposed frames, busted pipes, rotten food in refrigerators that hadn't had power for weeks, cupboards in which dry foods had been cooked by the heat and the moisture, cans that had swollen or burst. Insects and rodents roamed, gnawing and tearing what the fast-moving molds left behind. The inspectors were careful when they came calling: they wore face masks and gloves.

While hordes of photographers descended on the city, they mostly photographed the outside. There was plenty for them to document there: wind-torn and drowned houses, cars that ended up in trees, fishing boats thrown into buildings far from shore. There were also many close-ups of the anguished faces of New Orleanians of all ages, poignant portraits of suffering. New Orleans was, for at least six months after the Catastrophe, the most photographed city in the world. In fact, it was becoming the most over-photographed city in the world. After seeing so many images, we were in danger of becoming numb. Empathy comes easily when we are still close to the disaster, but as we move forward we begin to avert our eyes.

Burkholder understood intuitively that there was another world beyond the one with which we were becoming too visually familiar. It was there all the time, but it took something to see it rightly, and Burkholder had that something, mostly in his own way of seeing things, but also in the good luck and (necessary) serendipity of finding a new photographing technique that suited his vision. "Just weeks before my first trip to New Orleans," he tells us, "I began experimenting with a new kind of photography called high dynamic range (HDR) imaging . . . [that] lets photographers capture scenes with extremely high contrast ratios between the light and dark values. . . . Even rooms with glaringly bright windows and deep, dark shadows can now be rendered with visually inviting detail . . . for an almost painterly effect."

Burkholder, known primarily as a black-and-white photographer before going to New Orleans armed with HDR, found himself a world. He found, in the first place, the interiors of the city's abandoned houses where destruction had created environments of sinister beauty. He found the everyday objects of people's lives rearranged by wind and water, reconfigured by molds, torn and transformed by visible and invisible agents. A vivid and powerful life emanated from them.

In "Bookshelf Up Close," we meet someone's moldering library in an advanced stage of decay. The largest volume on the shelf has had its name obliterated by spots that look like a seated alien on the lower half and some sort of long-necked reptile at the top. These are Rohrschach figures, to be sure, but the book itself has become a mystery. I think that it may be the collected works of Victor Hugo, or Shakespeare's plays in one volume. Maybe. Does it matter? Yes, because other titles *can* still be read. *100 Great Operas* is still on one paperback spine, and we can also make out William Manchester's *A World Lit by Fire* and Daphne du Maurier's name on two different books. Who lived here? Someone I feel I know. Maybe. I don't know this person very well, because I'm no Daphne du Maurier fan, but it's someone I might have met and talked with, someone who reads literature. As far as readers go, New Orleans (like most cities) is a small town. This was a reader's library and that library is no more: all the books we see here will be thrown out, and the record of one reader's history will be erased. This reader, whoever she may be (I suspect it's a "she"), had taken great pleasure in her books, and that pleasure will now be tested. Despite the signs of destruction, the books still look cared for, their spines aligned by a caring hand. This reader will never recreate her library, this library, because even if she were to replace the titles, each of these books had a history that cannot be repeated. A true reader will go on to build a *different* library, but if she decides to repair and reinhabit the flooded house, the new books will take a long time to feel at home. They will feel the presence of the ghosts of the drowned books, and they could never, no matter how rich their content, inhabit the same physical space without feeling like thin, pale intruders. On the other hand, this reader may never return; this interior has been violated profoundly, beyond the violation of the mere objects, to the wellsprings of the mind that once understood the world through reading *these* books.

Dan Burkholder photographed this bookshelf several times. In another view, we cannot read the books' spines, leaving us with only the formal aspects of the ruination. The rich detail is still present—the deep colors of the molds still striking and sufficiently abstract to generate subjective shapes—but the titles are gone. Other objects are foregrounded: a clothes rack with shirts hanging from twisted hangers, an empty, fallen shelf. Other disappearing objects demand the photographer's eye: everything achieves equality in destruction. The books are not more important than the shirts, now that their functions are lost: the books can no longer be read; the shirts can no longer be worn. They all have one remaining material distinction: they are about to disappear into formlessness; they are equalized by uselessness. The bookshelf photographs tell a story, each view part of a narrative that can be read in any order the viewer chooses: from the intimate and readable portrait of the absent reader to the disappearing specificity of the bookshelf and the house succumbing to oblivion.

The bookshelf series is not the only narrative here; a whole series of pictures unfolds in church interiors. In the ironically titled "Church Exit Sign," we encounter a world of cracked mud, peeling wallpaper, a fallen light, and intact doors with stained glass windows under an EXIT sign, letting in light from the outside. There are layers of irony here, from the obvious EXIT sign in a place from which no one will exit any longer, to the survival of the stained glass windows amid the rubble. Someone might see divine intervention here, but it's a poor kind of intervention. The true wonders of this visual world are the cracked mud on the floor, which has taken an abundance of shapes, and the peeling walls that have become rich in shadows and deeply baroque in texture. A seeker of miracles would find in them much better evidence of a higher power. The unseen hands that wrought this creation have outdone any artist, even Jackson Pollock. The cracked floor gets the greater part of the photographer's attention in "Plant on Church Floor," a long shot of cracked mud between pews covered in cracked mud. At the end of the muddy vista is a gallery above the now barely visible EXIT doors. The plant noted in the title lies on its side in the foreground along with some seat cushions that have become art canvasses for molds. In "Church Pews," the perspective favors the curved beams of the ceiling, under which the listing and fallen pews appear, looking as if they were dramatically overturned by an angry force. Indeed, they have been, but this force was not the same flood that toppled the plant and the light in the other pictures. The flood had many faces, and the flood that caused the destruction in this image had something deliberate and operatic about it; it had a melodramatic face. It occurs to me that Dan Burkholder, who would probably deny it, couldn't help looking for some sign that all this destruction wasn't arbitrary.

That's human nature, whether you're looking through a photo lens or through tear-stained eyes. We all want to believe some intelligence operates within catastrophe, even if we know that it doesn't. This Catastrophe (like all natural events) was an equal-opportunity Destroyer: it slammed the rich and the poor, the bon vivants and the saints. But one can't help looking for some kind of intelligence, and here, Burkholder looks, editoralizing slightly.

In "Christ and Candles," he repents for it. Jesus stands in a large painting or print, fighting dark molds that have nearly overtaken the luminous gold of his robe and the blue sky above. The painting or print lies on the floor between two tables stacked with blue candles. The wall behind the tables is textured, primed, and full of potential images just waiting for the molds' next onslaught of self-expression to help them emerge. Here, there is no melodrama, just a simple acknowledgment that the agents of destruction are great artists, and even Jesus is no obstacle to their art if his surface is workable. "Stained Glass and Chairs" recapitulates both the melodrama and the exuberant randomness by means of two overturned chairs and an intact stained glass window of a post-resurrection Christ blessing the woman washing his feet. All objects here are closed claustrophobically between two narrow and richly textured walls. This church series is neither entirely ironic nor convincingly awe-filled, but it captures a certain hard-to-define feature of New Orleans: something religiously exalted amid a rotting cornucopia.

In fact, Dan Burkholder has captured New Orleans through her ruined objects in various ways. The objects belonged, of course, to the absent people of New Orleans, but the choice and arrangement of them, even the way they fell and decayed, speak to certain essences of the place. There are many antiques or older objects like Victorian lamps and clocks, Edwardian chairs, an old map of Louisiana, a red curtain (velvet?), and an entire "Funeral Home Fireplace" that exudes a kind of orderliness, even in the distribution of mud and debris. In New Orleans, one may see mud and molds behaving like delinquents in a church, but not in a funeral home. In the devastated kitchens, there is likewise something in the behavior of the destructive agents that might pass for thoughtfulness. The "Espresso Machine" retains the authority of its presence even amid the objects that have fallen on top of it and around it. A row of spoons stands sternly above a clogged sink, haughtily indifferent to the rising molds. (Can spoons be "haughty"? Yes, in New Orleans.) A kitchen cupboard, doors flung open, is crammed with dishes and glasses that look as if they were well used long before the Storm.

There are also social narratives: a series of photographs of the interior of a school is plainly sad. A row of mud-crusted coppery lockers floats on the remnants of what used to be the floor; the lone open locker reveals a football helmet. The "Shoe and Gym Bag in the Mud" likewise bespeaks a wounded young life. The "Water Fountain in Locker Room" is covered with shards of mud, each one as well defined as a fragment of ancient pottery. No need for comment here. There are also images of what might have been a Black or Creole house, judging by the art fallen from the wall and the video of *Roots* lying in front of the red curtain. For the most part, however, these vague social narratives are without strong content. There is little discernible difference between the rich and the poor whose dying objects Burkholder photographed. The very few times that these interiors include an open window, or a doorway, we do not see anything specific through this opening: the outside looks generic.

There are other aspects to Burkholder's project, one in particular that is so subversive it might seem callous. I don't think it is, but then I am an artist, and this aspect of Burkholder's work is what I call the Art Project. Many of his images aim consciously or unconsciously to recall certain art periods. There is a kind of "history of art" running through them. The abstractions of cracked mud and humidity-deconstructed walls are tended to with painterly dedication. The racks of hanging shirts in "Clothes in Green Room" and hanging robes in "Green Choir Robes" are reminiscent of New York pop artist Jim Dine's work. The perspective in "Arched Door" is Dalinian. There is a constructivist mural-like composition in "School Heating Plant." Pop Art and Expressionism hover pointedly in places, and there are glosses on paintings from El Greco to Georges Braques. It is entirely possible that Burkholder's camera had no choice, because the camera is a postmodern device par excellence: it captures not only what's there in front of it, but also what's there in the image bank of the beholder. It is also possible that Burkholder had more fun than he intended to—but this Art Project does not diminish the pathos evident in his images, nor the suffering that they imply.

The wonder of these photographs is that they look like paintings, yet the objects depicted within them are not idealized. The dying domestic objects of the people to whom these interiors belong are no longer of this world. They have been captured on their journey to becoming indistinct trash. At the moment of their capture, they still looked like what they used to be, but moments after they were photographed, they no longer were anything. Their last breath of life is in these photographs; their only other existence is in the memories of their owners. The style of Burkholder's photographic essay both resembles and opposes Victorian funerary photography. The Victorians liked pictures of their departed ones resting on catafalques or deathbeds, dressed in their best clothes, exuding order and serenity. Burkholder's content couldn't be more different: everything is disorder, chaos, disruption—and rich chromatic beauty. The engraving quality of the prints reminds us, perversely, of wedding invitations and other solemn announcements, raising again the paradoxical question of the connection between Catastrophe and Art. Meanwhile, Dan Burkholder has, without question, immersed himself and us in an unrepeatable vision.

Andrei Codrescu is the author of Wakefield, *a novel, and* it was today: new poems. *He has written extensively about photography, including two essays on Walker Evans published by the Getty Museum.*

Shadows of Lives and Loss

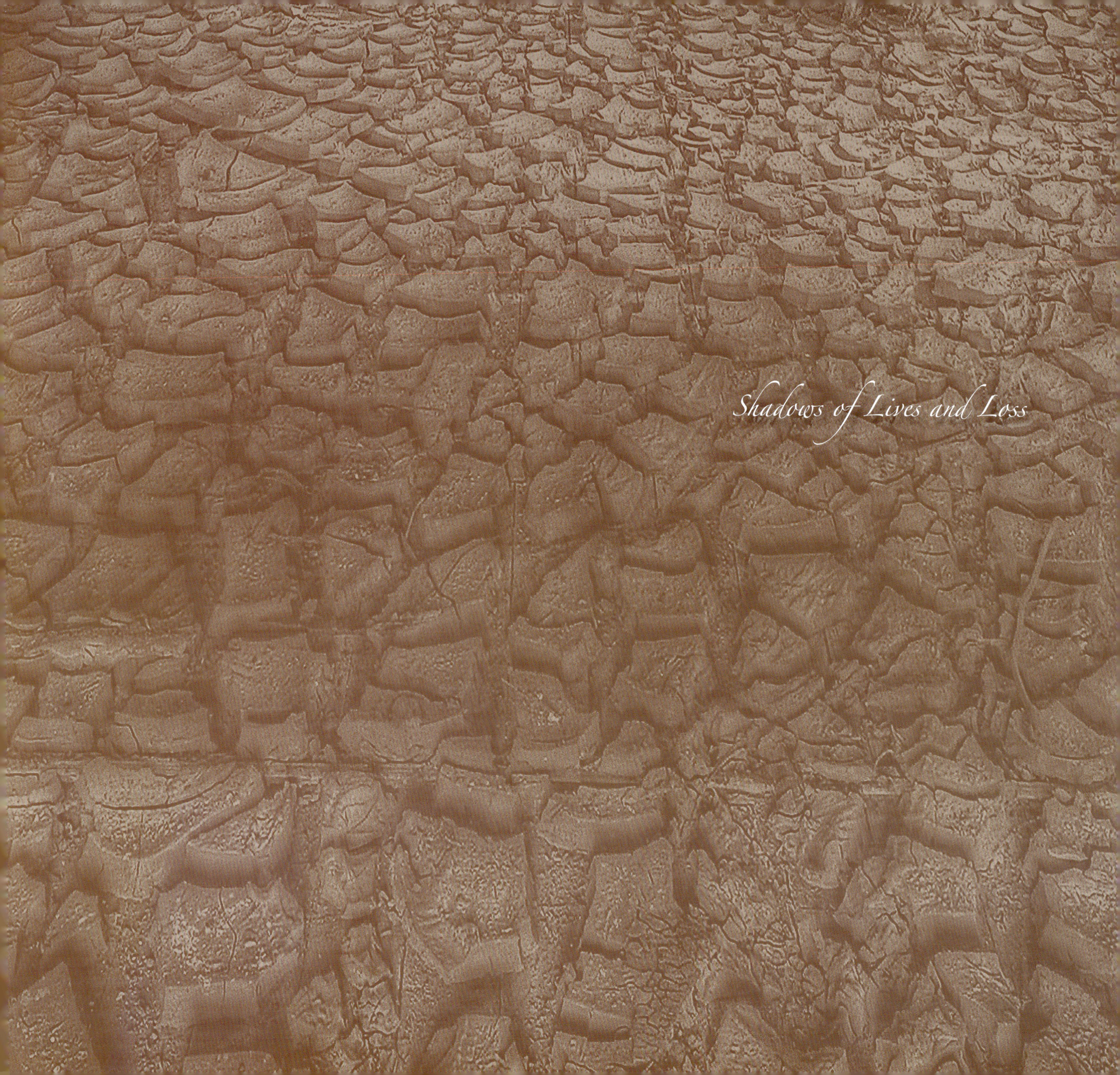

When Hurricane Katrina smashed into New Orleans I was teaching a photography workshop in Montana, nestled comfortably in the cool, green mountains of the Northwest. It would be hard to imagine an environment more sociologically, aesthetically, or emotionally separated from the events that were taking place on our Gulf Coast. As images of the catastrophe filled the television screen, it was difficult to pull myself away. Invariably, the TV and magazine articles focused on the *outside* world of destruction. Pictures of the breached levee, houses on top of other houses, and cars in trees quickly became iconic visuals for the event. Still, I couldn't help but feel that a more important story of individual loss was being missed. As shocking as the flooding was to witness via video and print, there was a distance and anonymity to the images in the news.

I didn't immediately know I'd be making a pilgrimage to New Orleans to see and photograph what was left of the city. A festering awareness finally came to a head in early 2006 and I realized I had to go see for myself what had happened to her citizens. When I first set foot in the flooded sections of New Orleans, I saw immediately that a more personal and intimate story was hidden away where few camera crews had ventured. This larger and even more compelling story was lurking inside the homes, schools, businesses, and churches of New Orleans, and I began to document it. I think of the resulting photographs as *portraits without people,* in which the soul and spirit of the residents of New Orleans are more evident and essential than in the piles of litter in the streets outside.

One of the first things you will notice in this book is that the camera never ventures outdoors. You will occasionally get a glimpse of the outside world through a window or an open doorway, but your vantage point is always from within the clutter and dirt of damaged interiors. More than one friend or colleague encouraged me to take additional photos outside in the streets. It will make for a more complete photo essay, they said. No, I responded; others would do that job.

I took photographic liberties with this series of images, for several reasons. We are constantly bombarded with photographic depictions, via TV, web, and print, of everything from commercial products to disaster coverage. The result is that we easily become bored and perceptually complacent. I call this reaction to the overload of images "visual immunity." To avoid producing this response, one of my photographic goals was to capture the city's interiors more intensely and more poetically than a pure documentary approach would allow.

Employing photographic techniques that emphasized detail was critical. The visual tableau was vastly different from anything I'd seen before, largely because the flooding in New Orleans was so unparalleled. Weeks of soaking in filthy saltwater had changed everyday items into uncanny archaeological artifacts. The cracked mud, the corrosion on metal objects, the curling of wallpaper, the pink insulation drooping from ceilings—everywhere I looked there was another shocking detail to be recorded and highlighted. No matter how I photographed the interiors, it was important that this detail not only be captured, but also be rendered with rich texture and dimension.

Another primary photographic decision was to shoot in color. Though I'd worked for years as a black-and-white photographer, it was immediately obvious to me that New Orleans had to be portrayed in color, and confident color at that. In homes, businesses, churches, and schools, you'll see how boldly the residents of New Orleans embrace color in their surroundings. A monochromatic interpretation would have done a disservice to those rich choices.

Sometimes the way life's events are arranged works to our advantage. Just weeks before my first trip to New Orleans, I began experimenting with a new kind of photography called high dynamic range (HDR) imaging. In a nutshell, a judicious use of hardware and software lets photographers capture scenes with extremely high contrast ratios between the light and dark values. Had I tried to photograph settings similar to those depicted in this book a few years earlier, I'd have been forced to walk away from many of the subjects. There was no way a single exposure on film or digital chip could capture the extreme range of brightness values. HDR has changed all of that. Even rooms with glaringly bright windows and deep, dark shadows can now be rendered with visually inviting detail in every part of the image, for an almost painterly effect. HDR imaging was the perfect tool for capturing the harshly lit interiors of flood-ravaged New Orleans.

Note that HDR images look different from "normal" photographs. If an image appears overly colorful to your eye, it's not because I artificially accentuated the colors with Photoshop®, but rather because so much color is revealed by the HDR process. Shadows that would otherwise appear dark and empty are now open and full of color; highlights that would be washed out and blank are richly textured and color filled. Your eye discovers information in every part of the image.

Using color and HDR techniques together revealed detail and captured the breadth of destruction, but by themselves they would not have been enough to make successful photographs. It has been said that placement of the camera is one of the most important decisions a photographer makes. With only a few exceptions, for the photos in this book I positioned the camera at eye level. I hope this helps you, the viewer, experience a "you are there" point of view. As you look at each image, you should feel as though you just walked into the room and are seeing the destruction for the first time. Scan the room and imagine standing in someone's home, now a wreck awaiting the bulldozer.

For those interested in such technical issues, the longest focal length used (on a full-size chip DSLR) was 24mm; most images in the series were exposed with an ultra-wide zoom between 12 and 15MM. You will notice lots of perspective effects in the photos. When the camera looks down, vertical lines converge. The point wasn't to distort, but rather to present a more intimate interpretation than longer lenses would offer. I feel that the vertical convergence you see in many of the photos adds to the sense of disarray and confusion, better typifying the scenes that were before the camera.

It is important to convey that I approached this project as an artist, photographer, and humanitarian rather than as a journalist. I unabashedly used photographic techniques that produced a hyper-real rendition of the carnage, going far beyond a straight portrayal. One of photography's jobs is to distill visual understanding from chaos and disarray—that is, to create a scene that gives your imagination the capacity to pause and explore, then to comprehend. Some who have seen this series feel I have overprocessed the images, or that they look more like paintings than photographs. I suspect that those viewers, more often than not, are uncomfortable with their attraction to the images, feeling guilt that photographs representing such terrible misfortune can actually have a visual intrigue and appeal. Trust me, if I didn't feel the approach matched the subject matter and the conditions perfectly, I would have photographed another way, or not at all. These are detailed photographs that invite inspection; this isn't an accident. My sincerest hope is that the captured minutiae give you a more personal experience as you witness the havoc thrust upon the people of New Orleans.

There is nothing pretty about the aftermath of Hurricane Katrina: certainly not the lives it claimed, the city it changed forever, nor the property that was lost. For decades I've declared my photographic devotion to emotional honesty over literal honesty. These photographs are, for me, the most emotionally accurate portrayal I can possibly share with you, the reader. For those unable or unwilling to make the journey to the Lower Ninth Ward and other heavily damaged parts of New Orleans, I offer this book so that you too can witness the shadows of lives and loss in the Crescent City.

DAN BURKHOLDER
2007

The Photographs

Wagon and Window

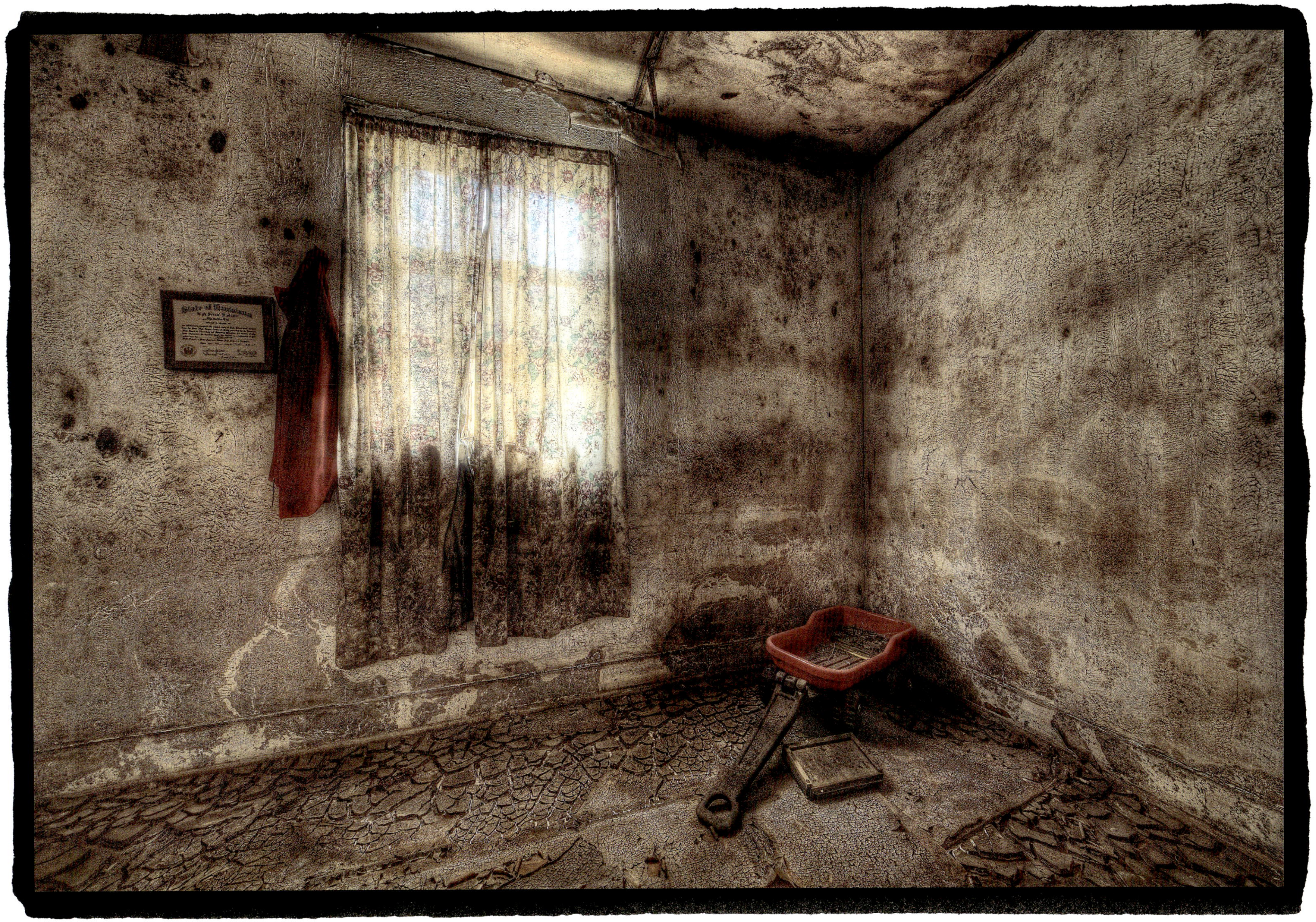

Framed Print and Bookcases

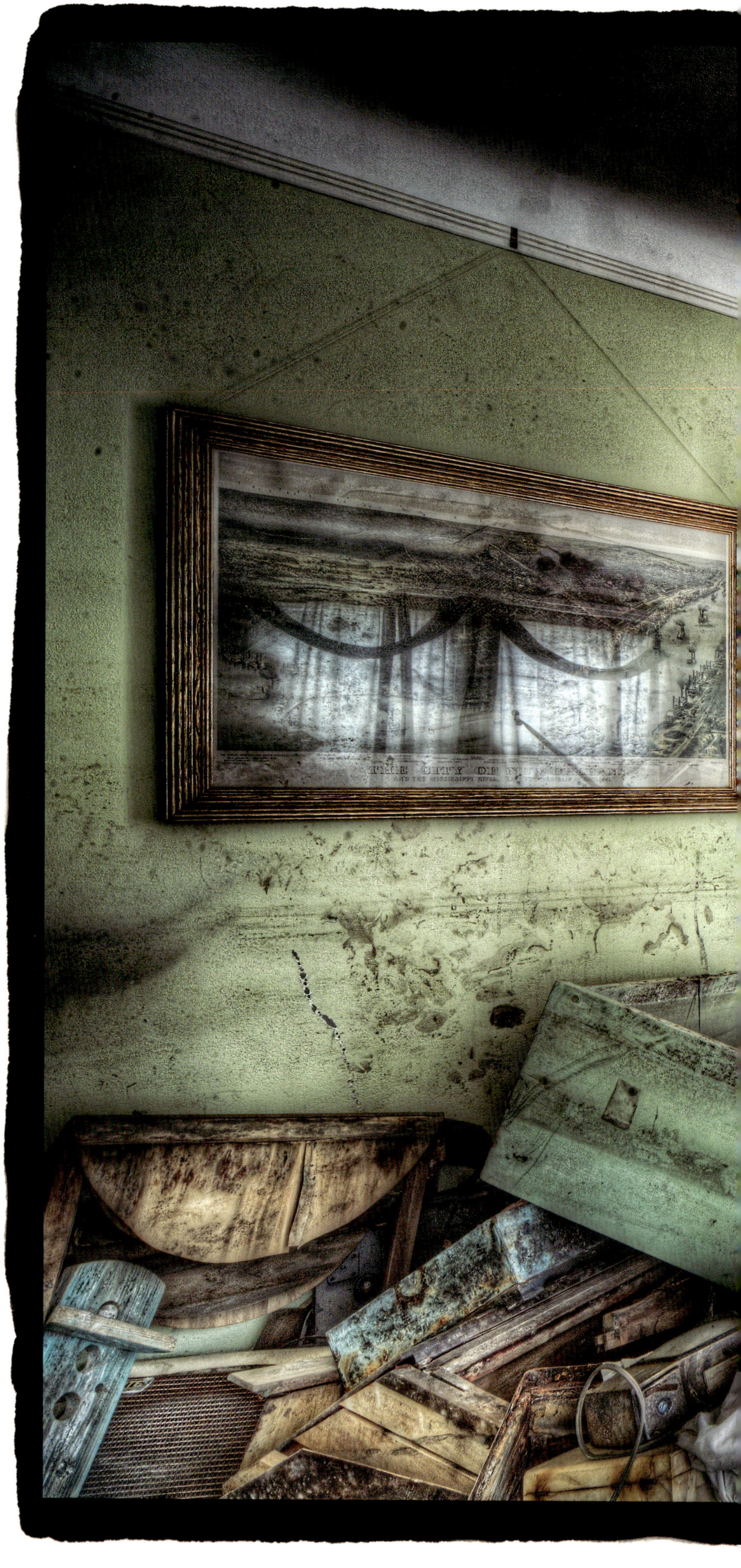

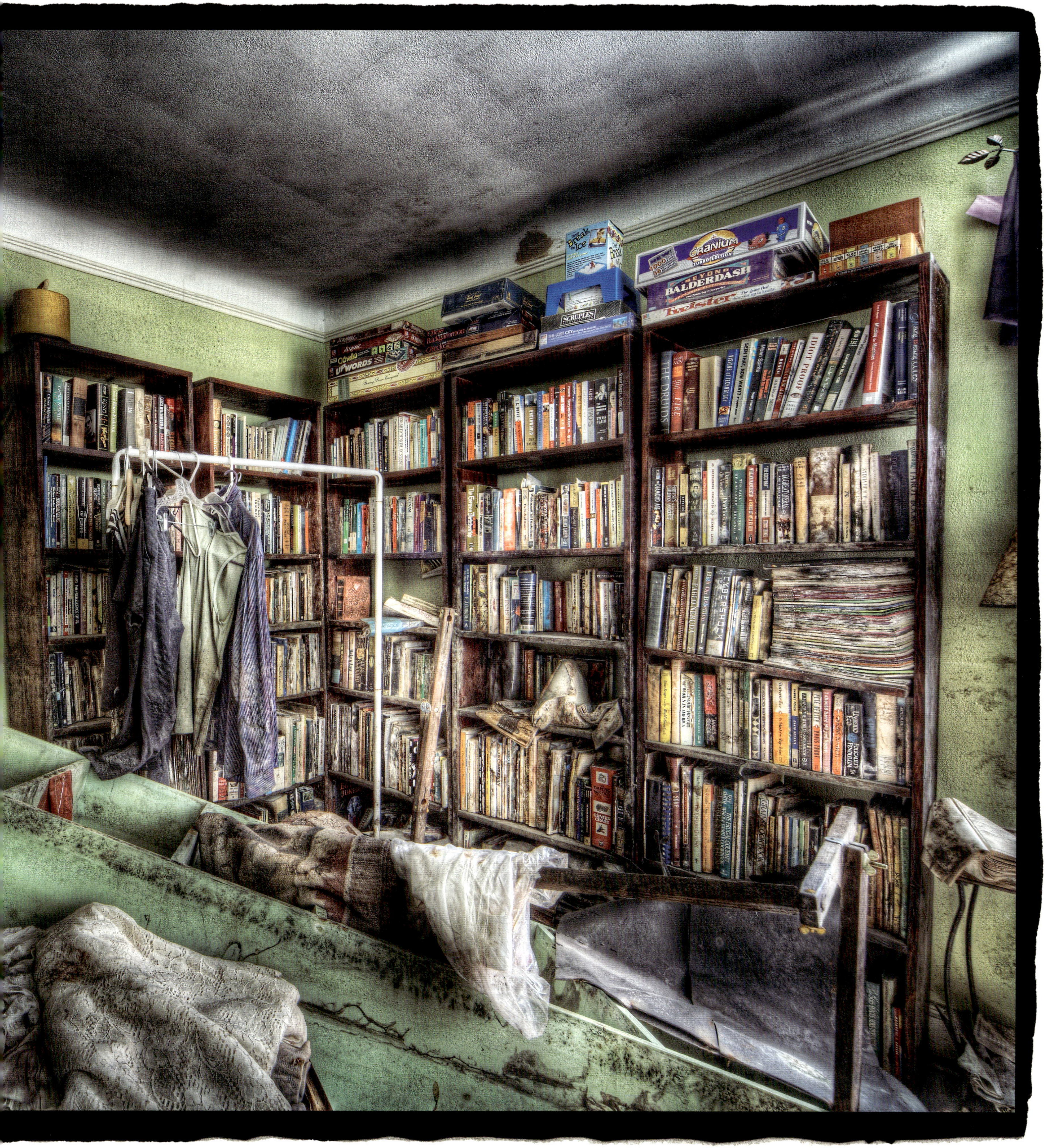
CRANIUM
BEYOND
BALDERDASH
SCRUPLES
UPWORDS
IDIOT PROOF
THE DRUIDS

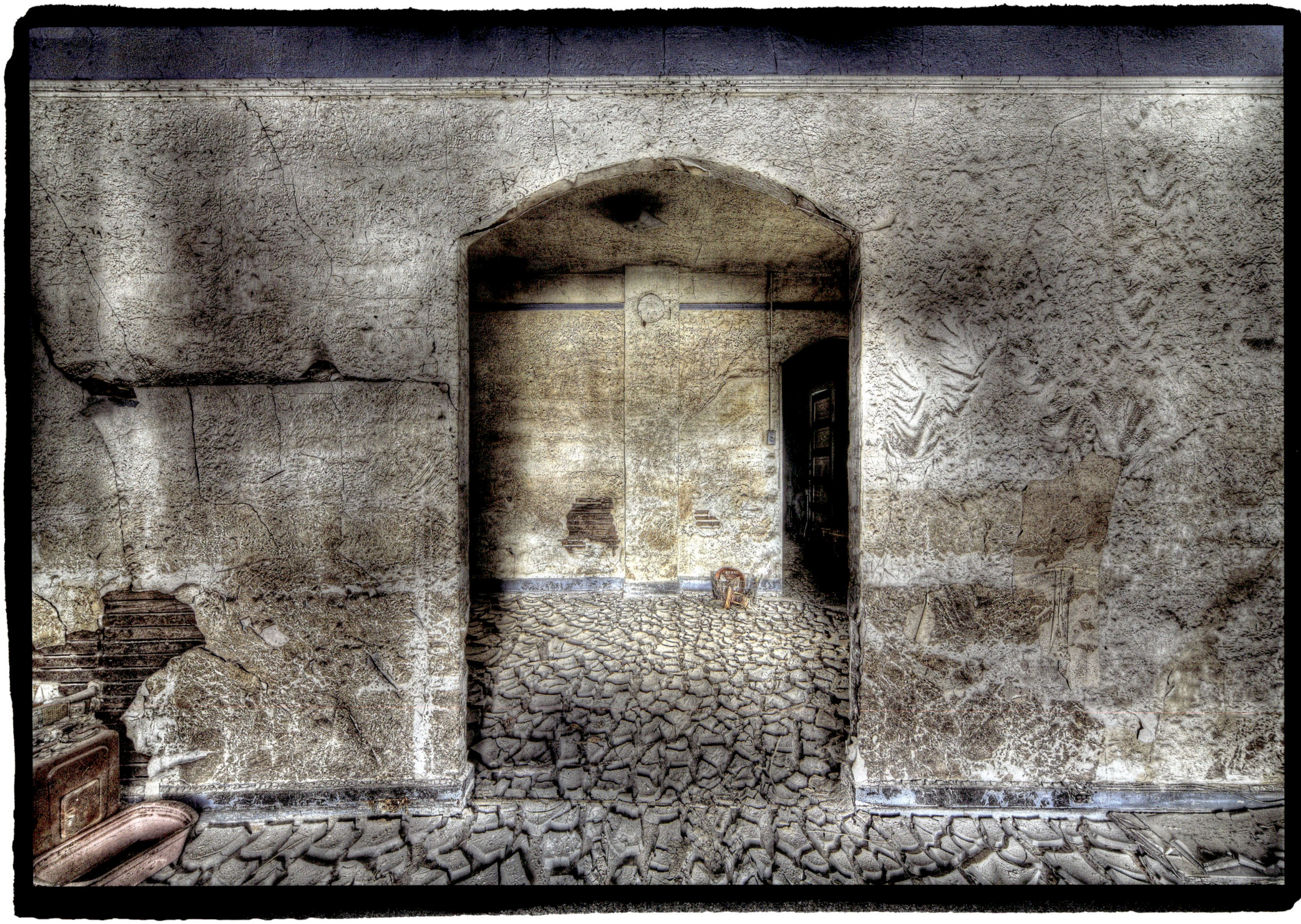

Arched Door

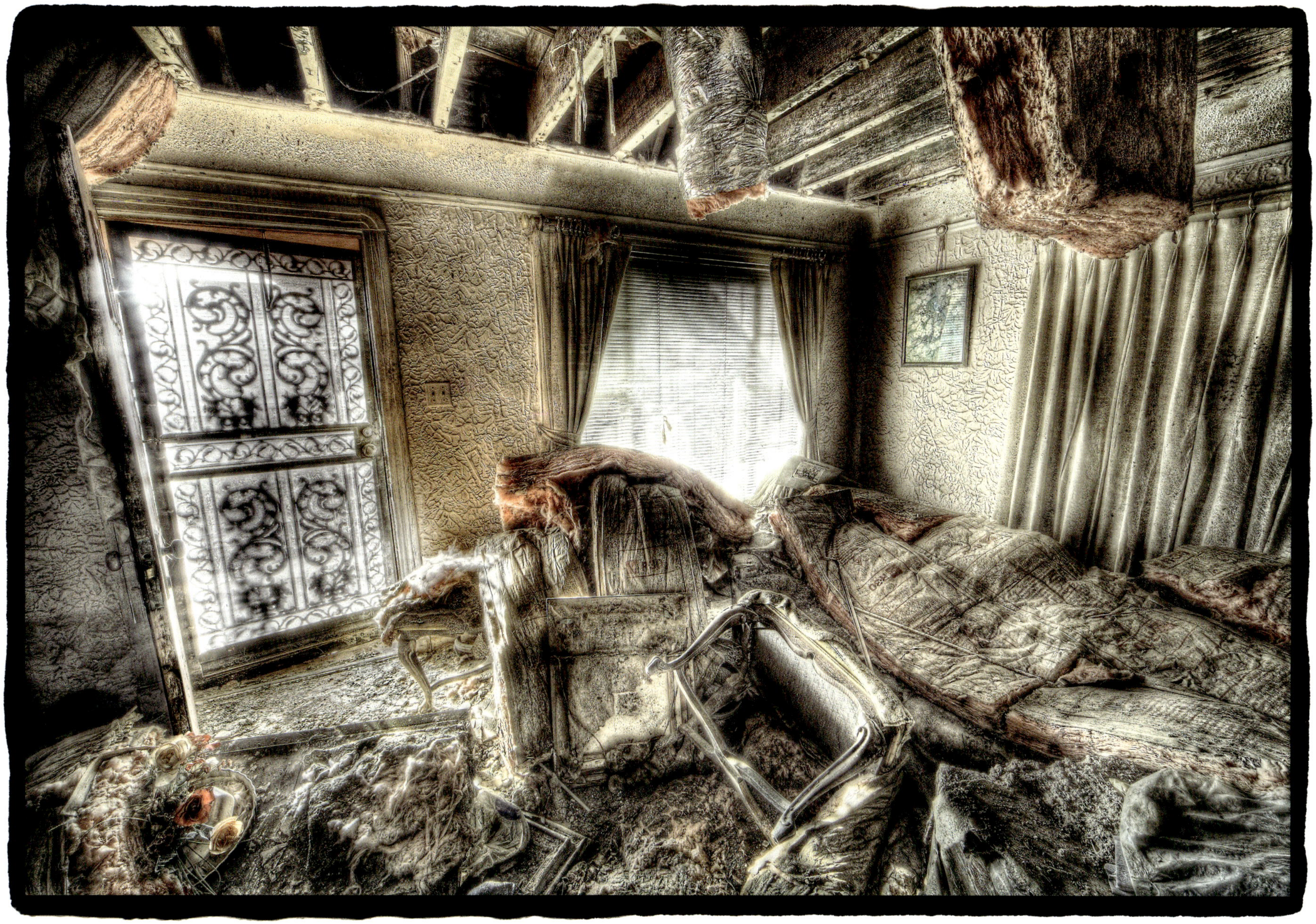

Door with Grate

Fireplace in Blue Room

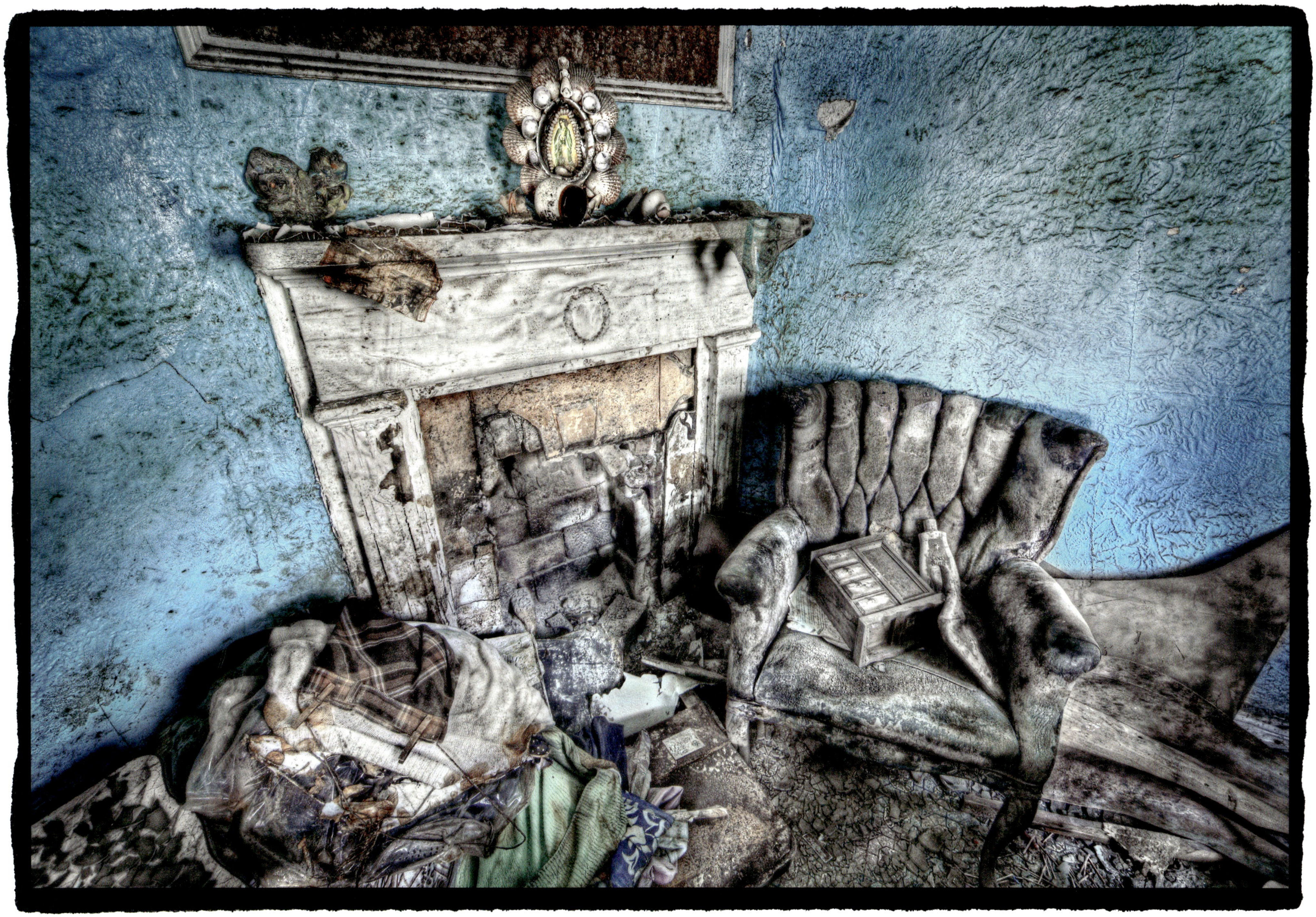

Fish Tank

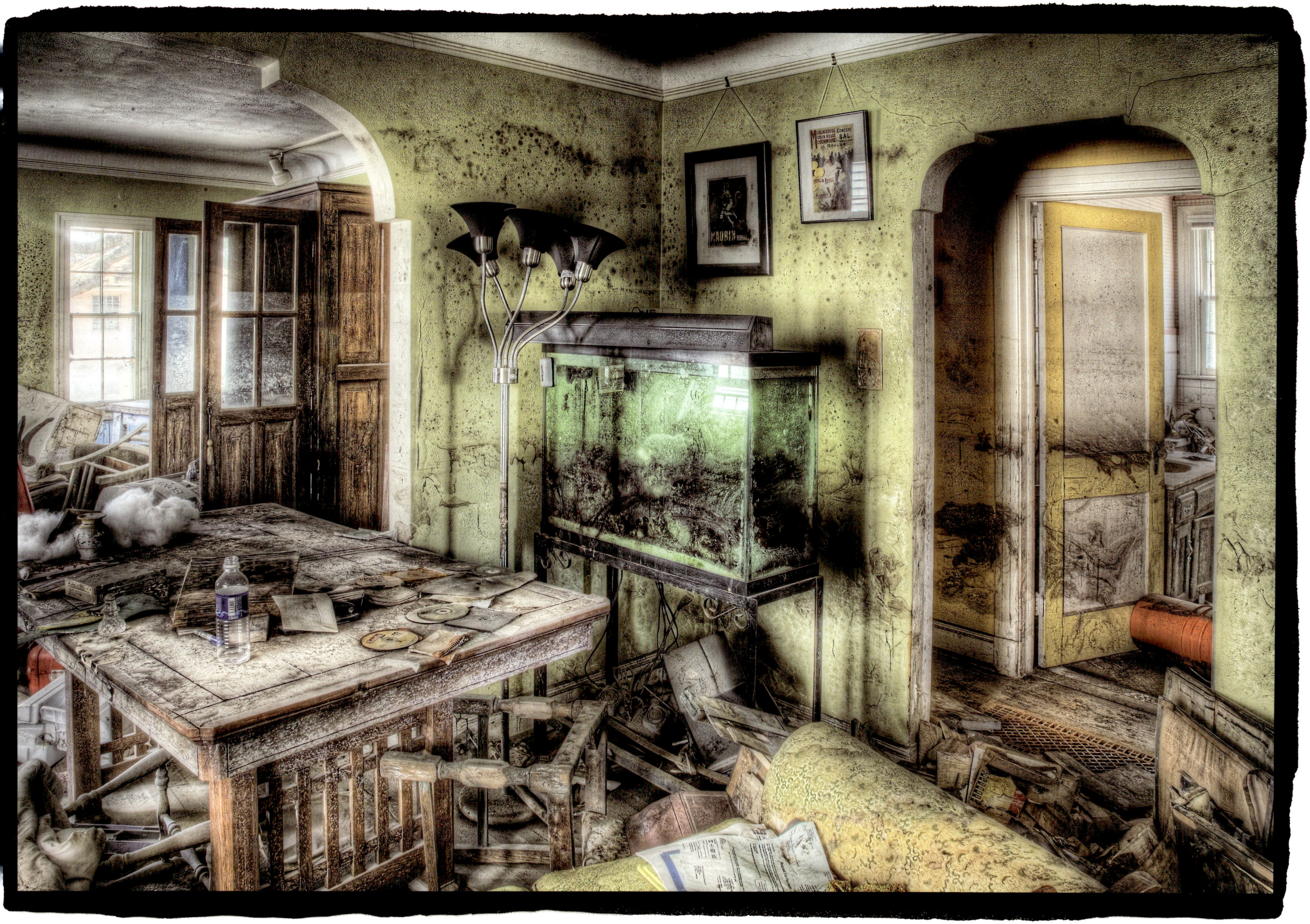

Insulation on Bed

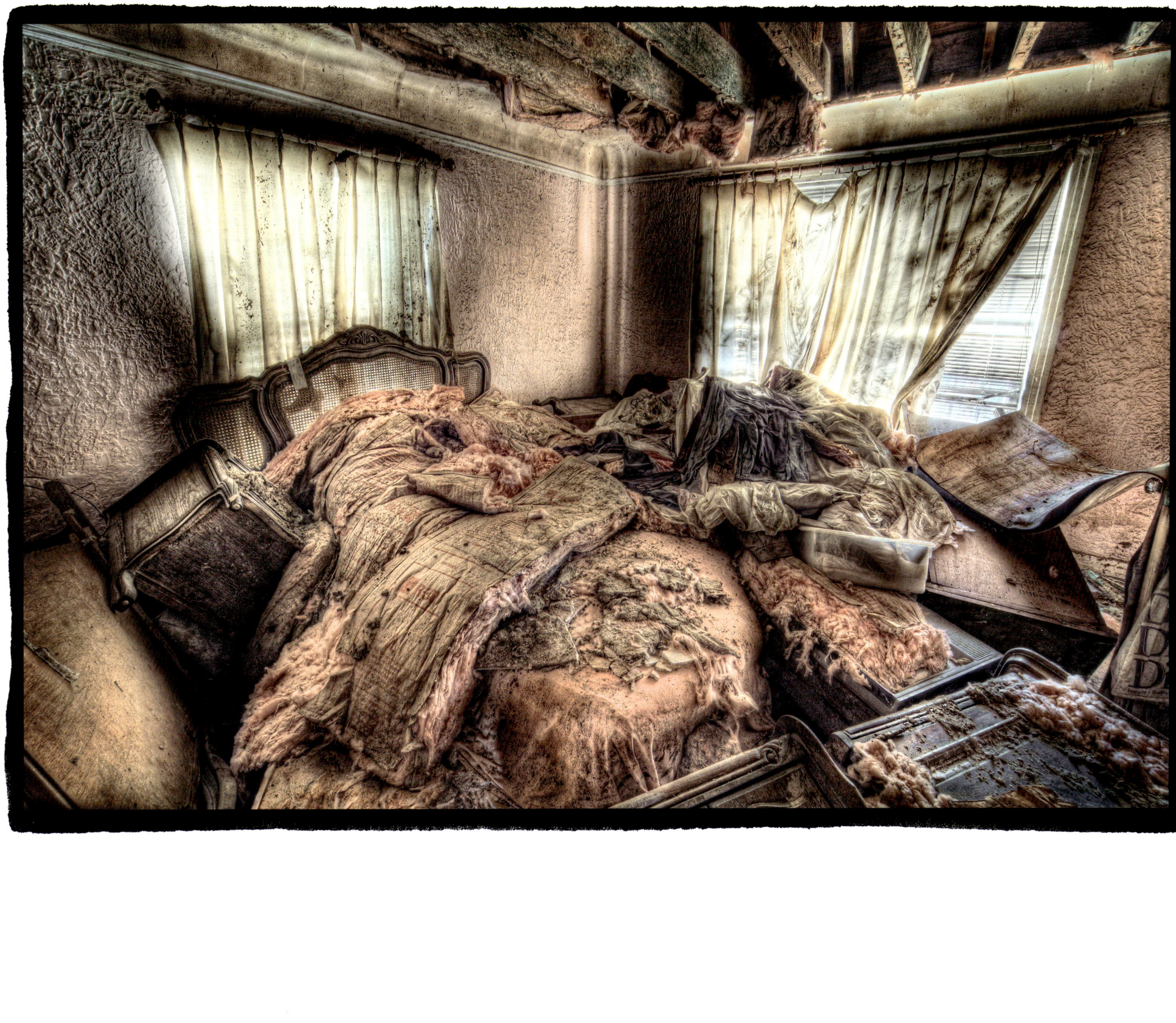

Map of Louisiana

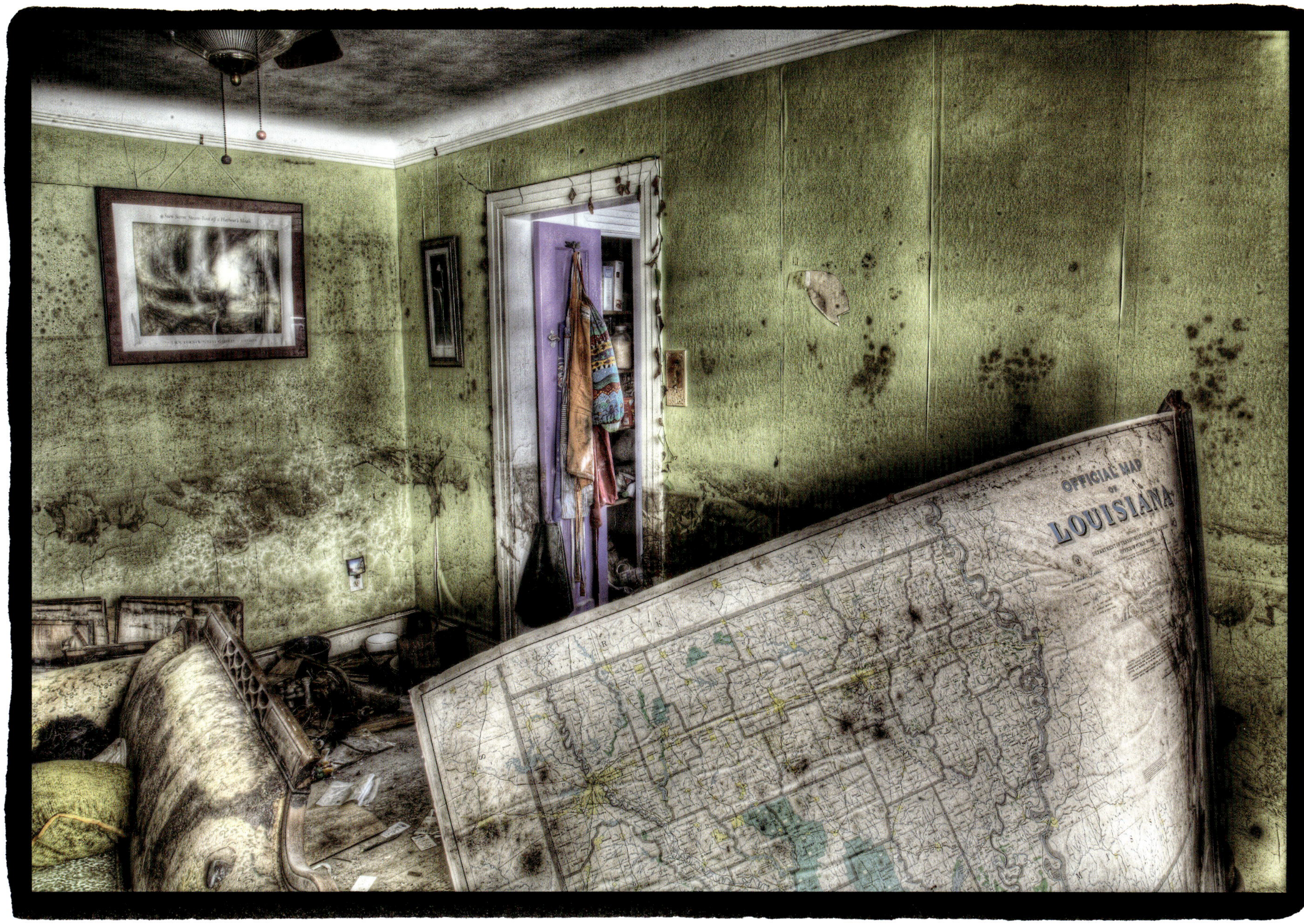
OFFICIAL MAP
LOUISIANA

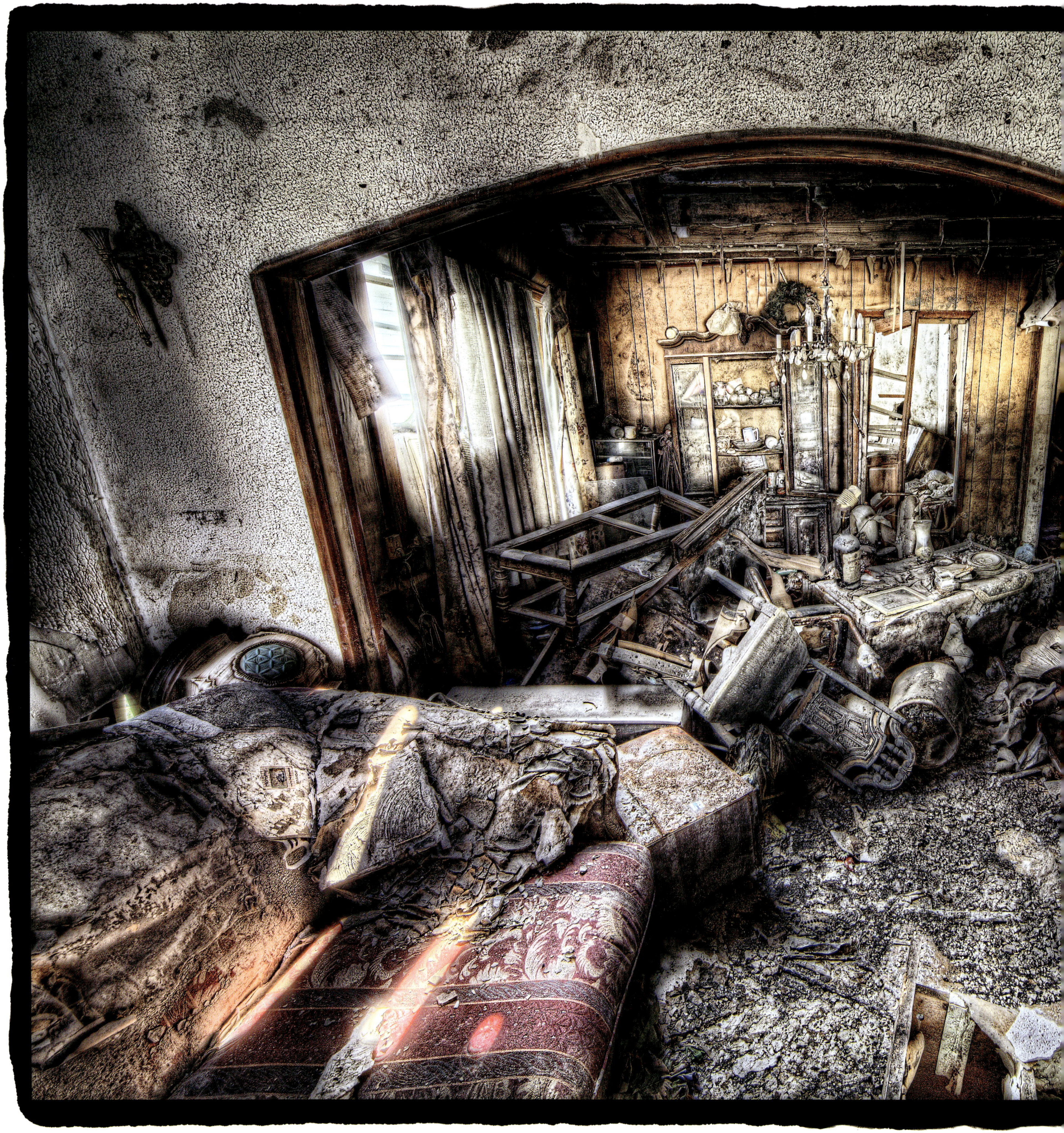

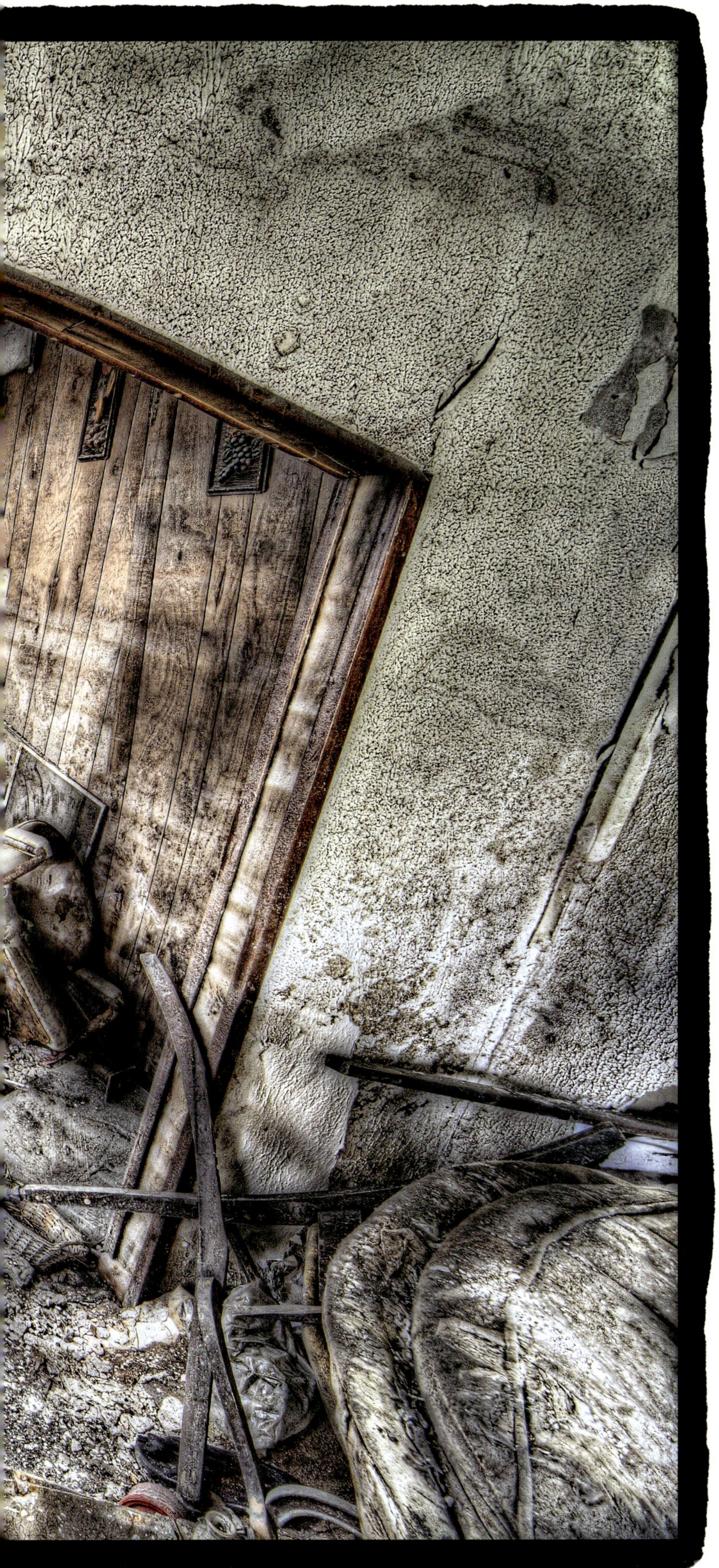

Arch and Dining Room

Sunroom

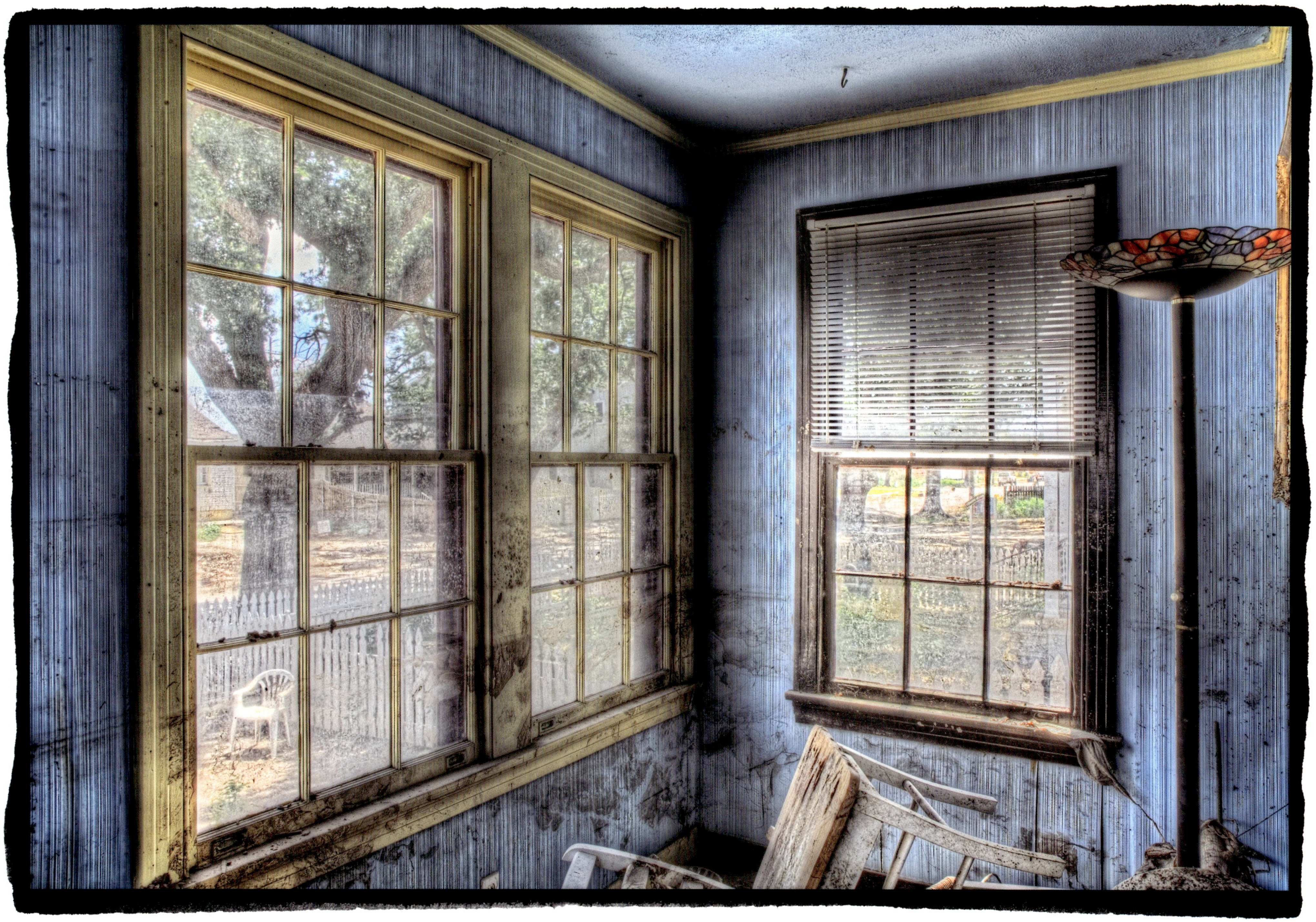

Living Room and Levee

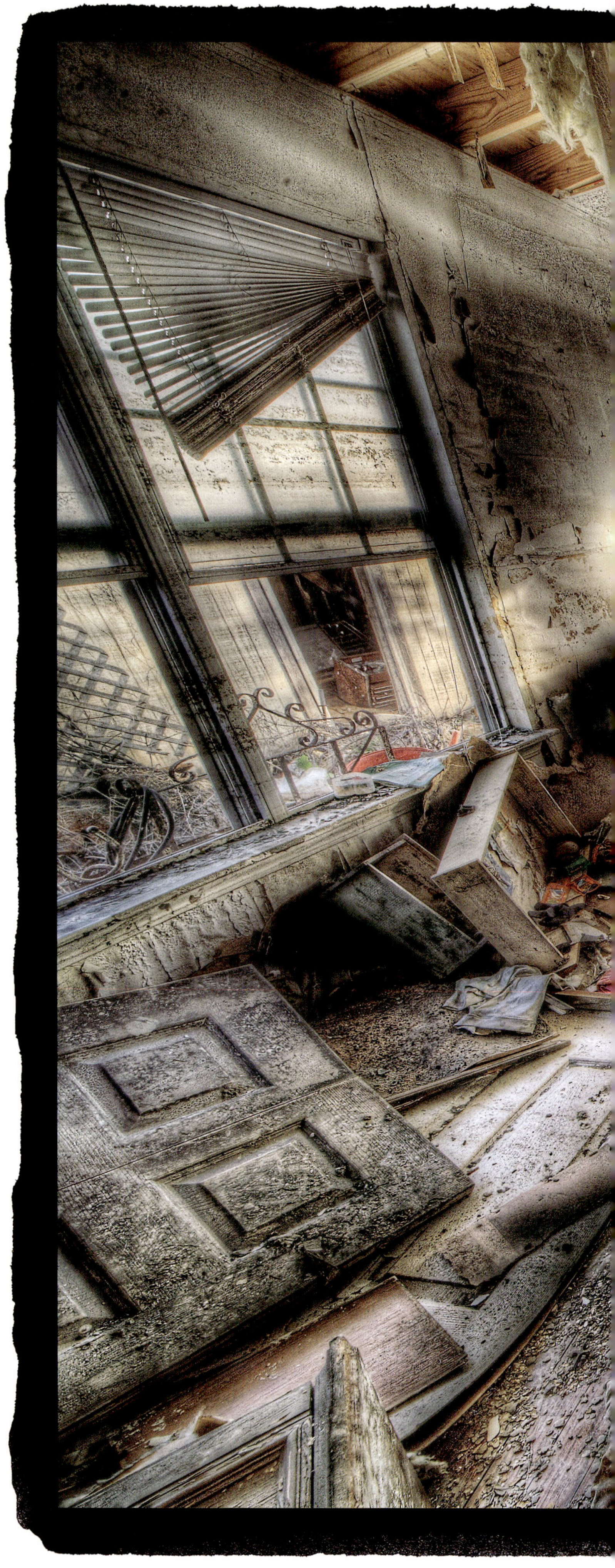

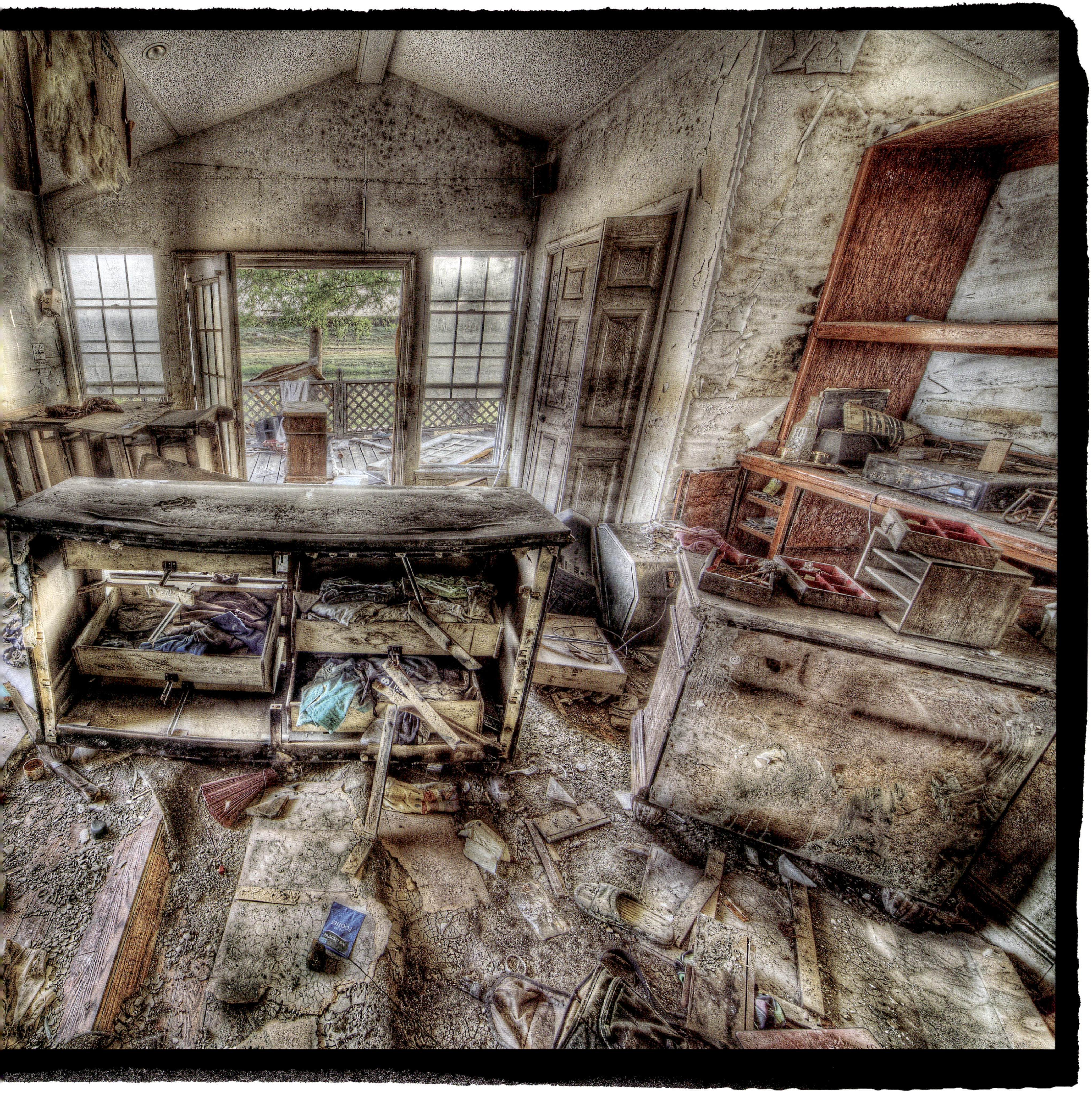

Nested Doorways

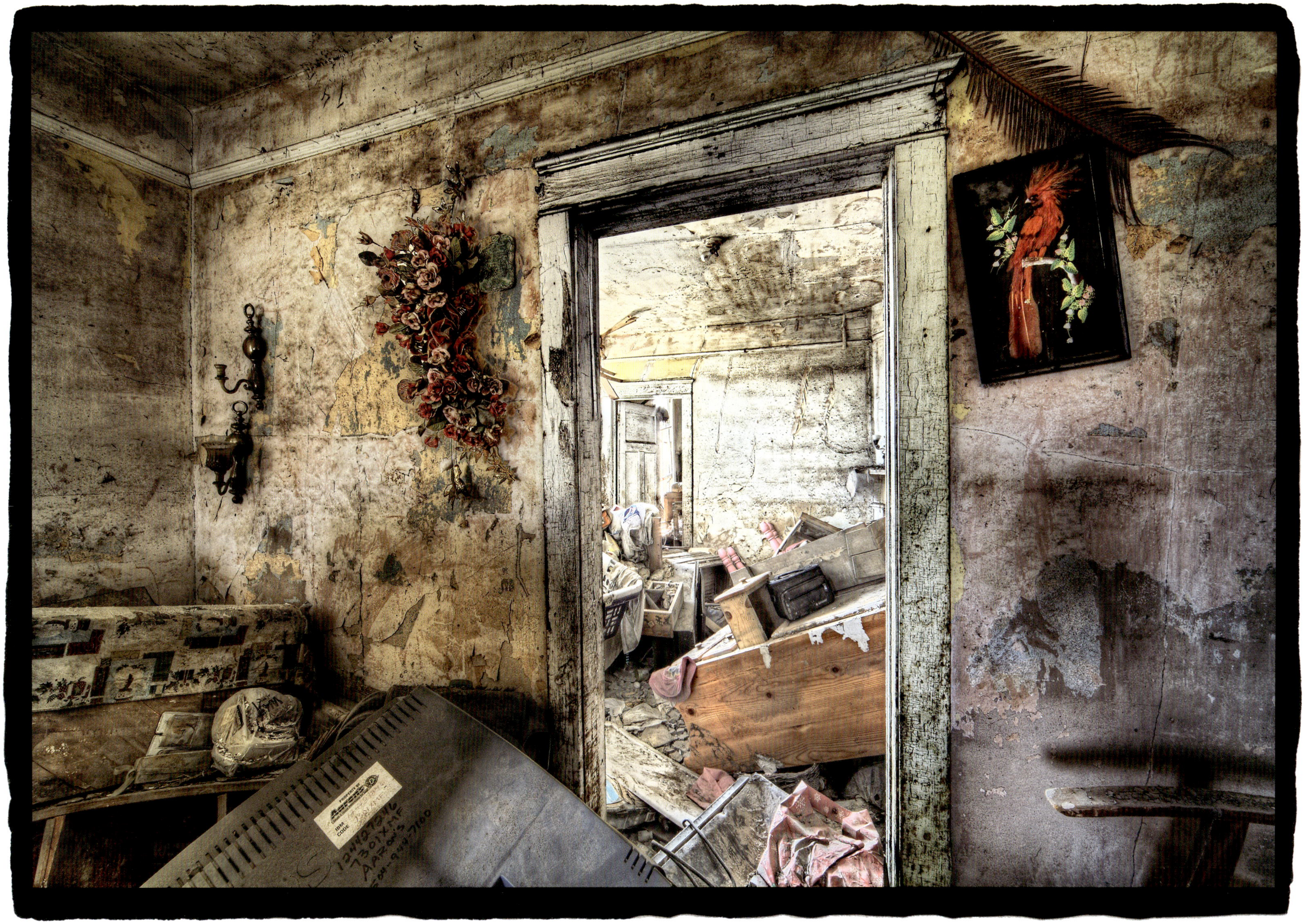

Open Chest in Bedroom

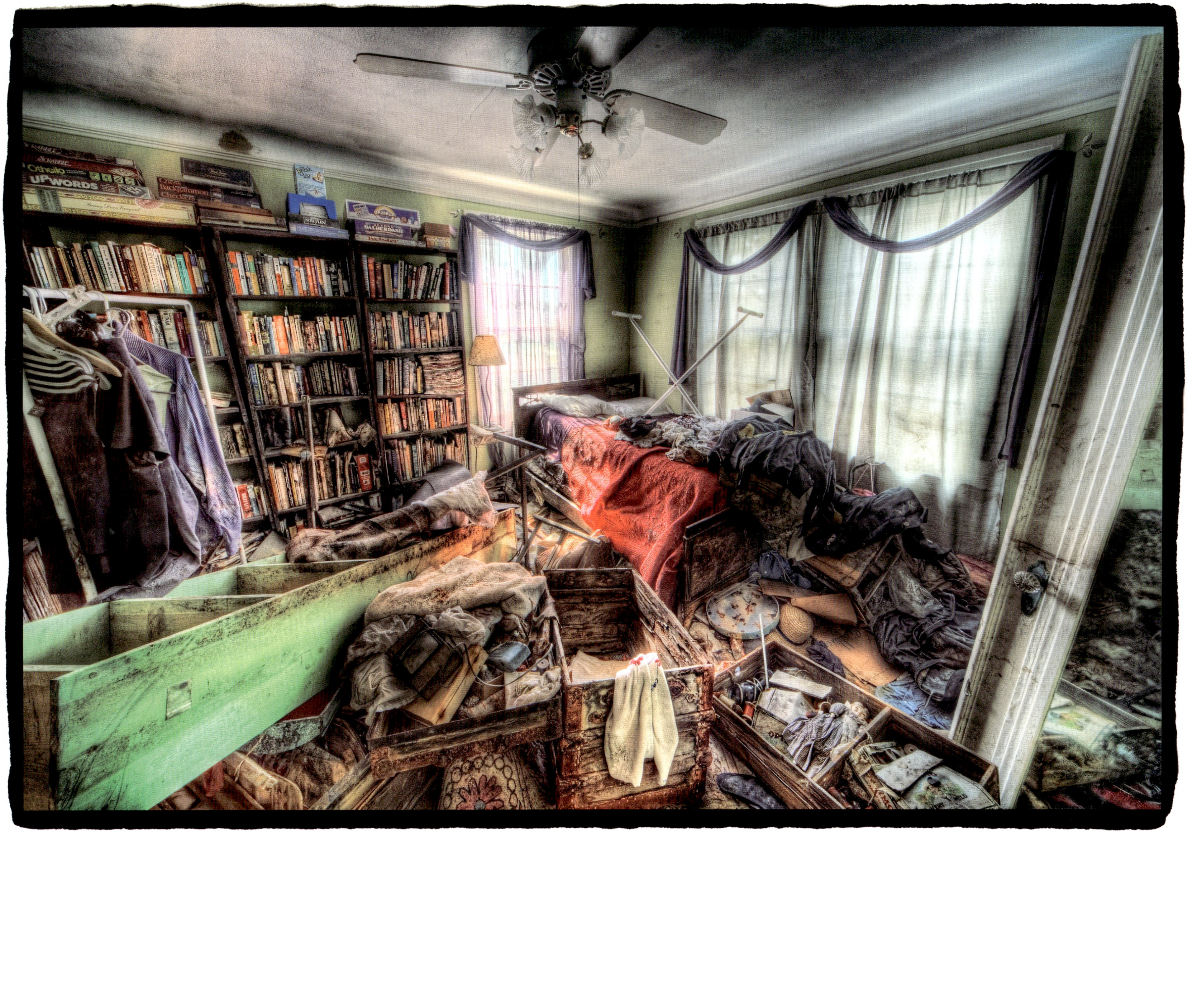

Othello
UPWORDS
Chess
Backgammon
Checkers
SCRUPLES
BALDERDASH

Open Kitchen Door

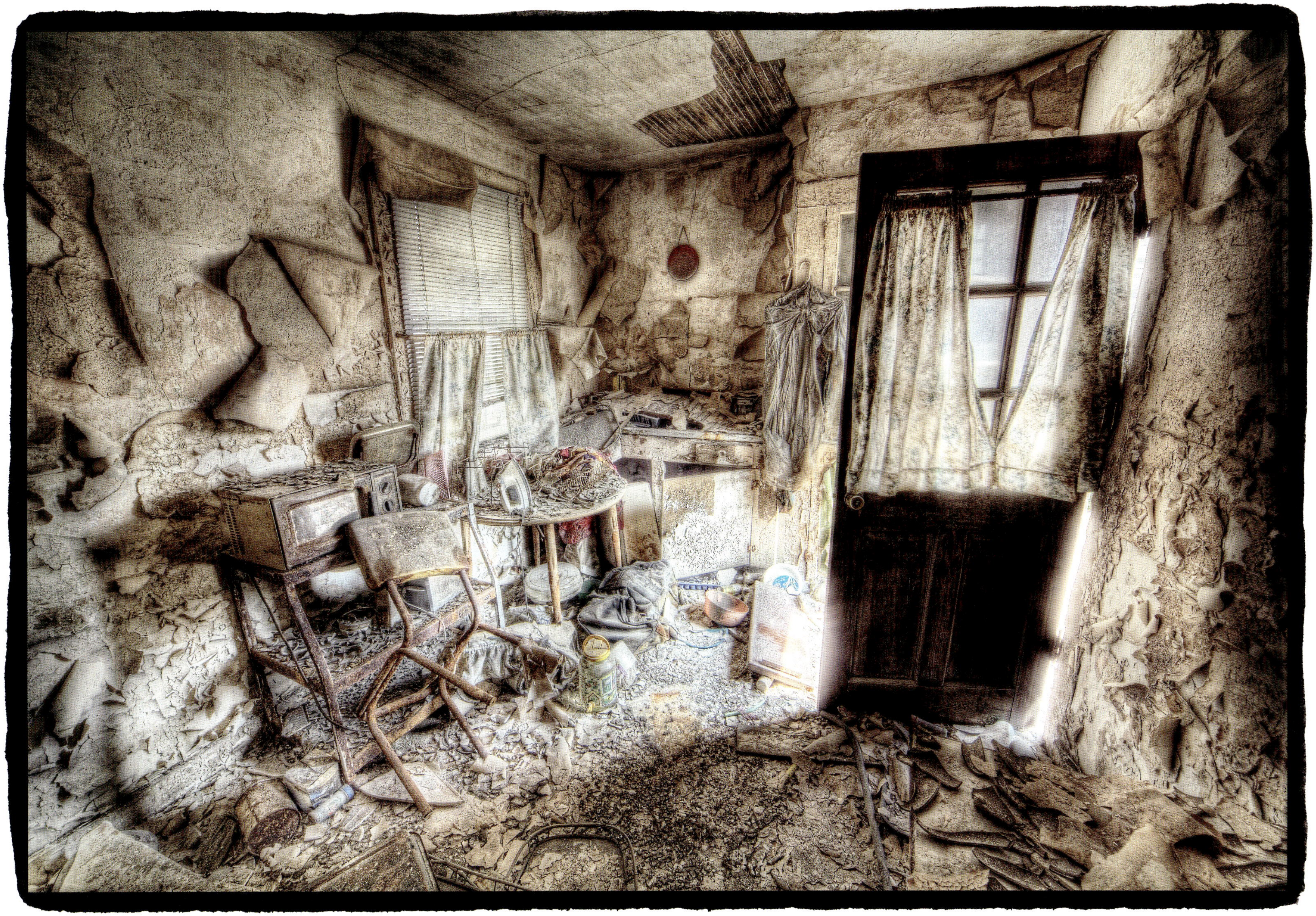

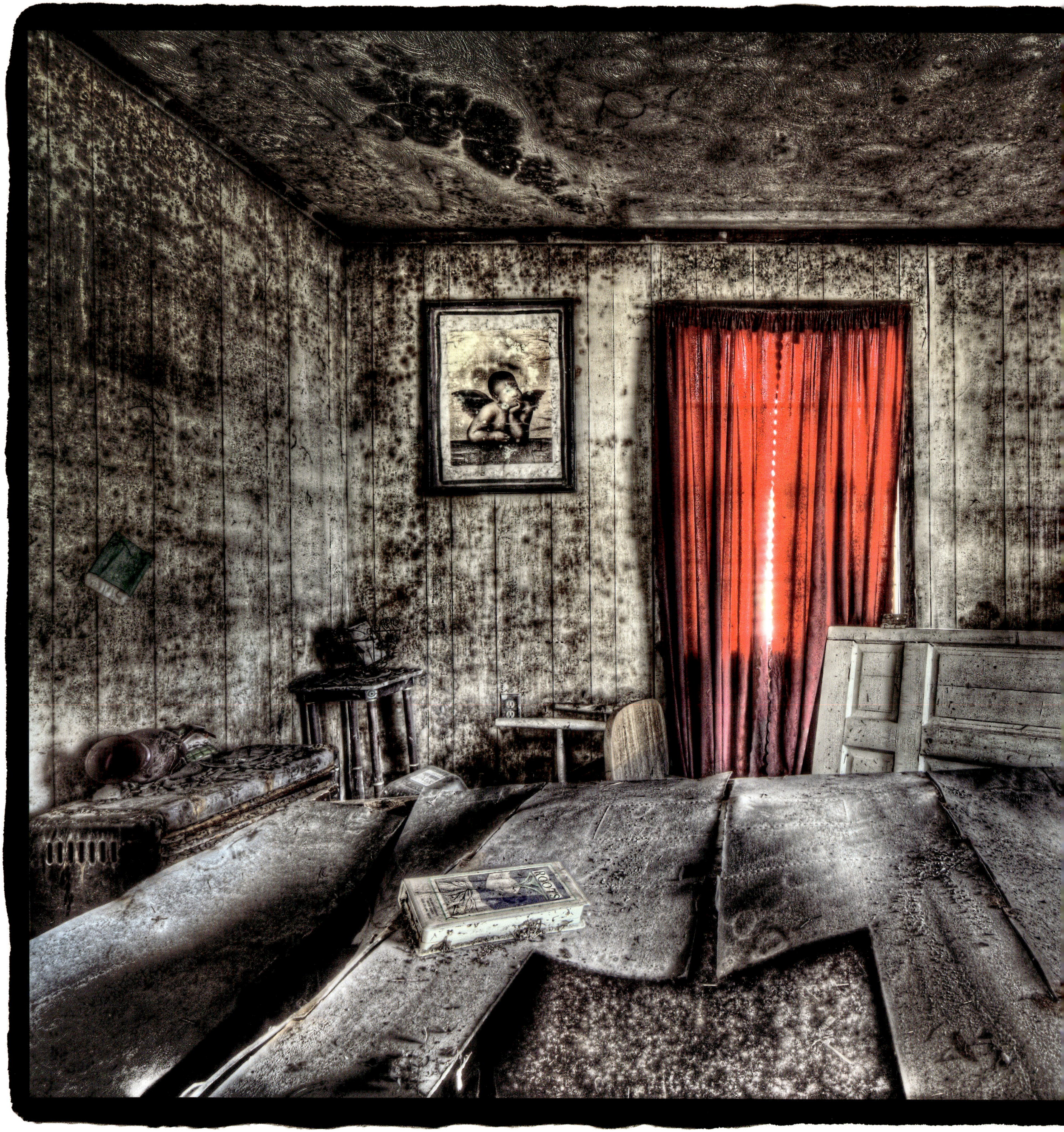
ROOTS

Red Curtain and "Roots" Video

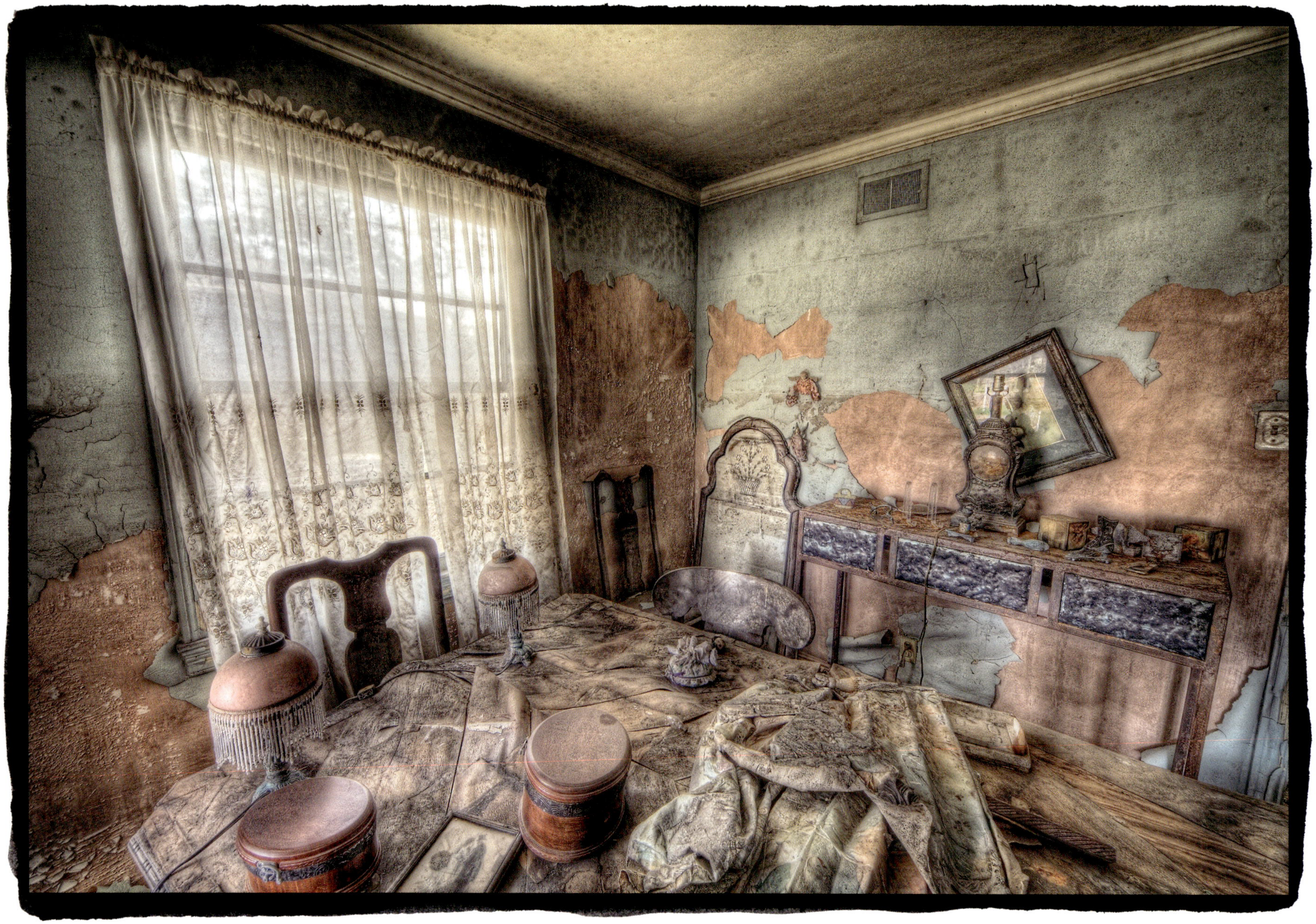

Table and Window

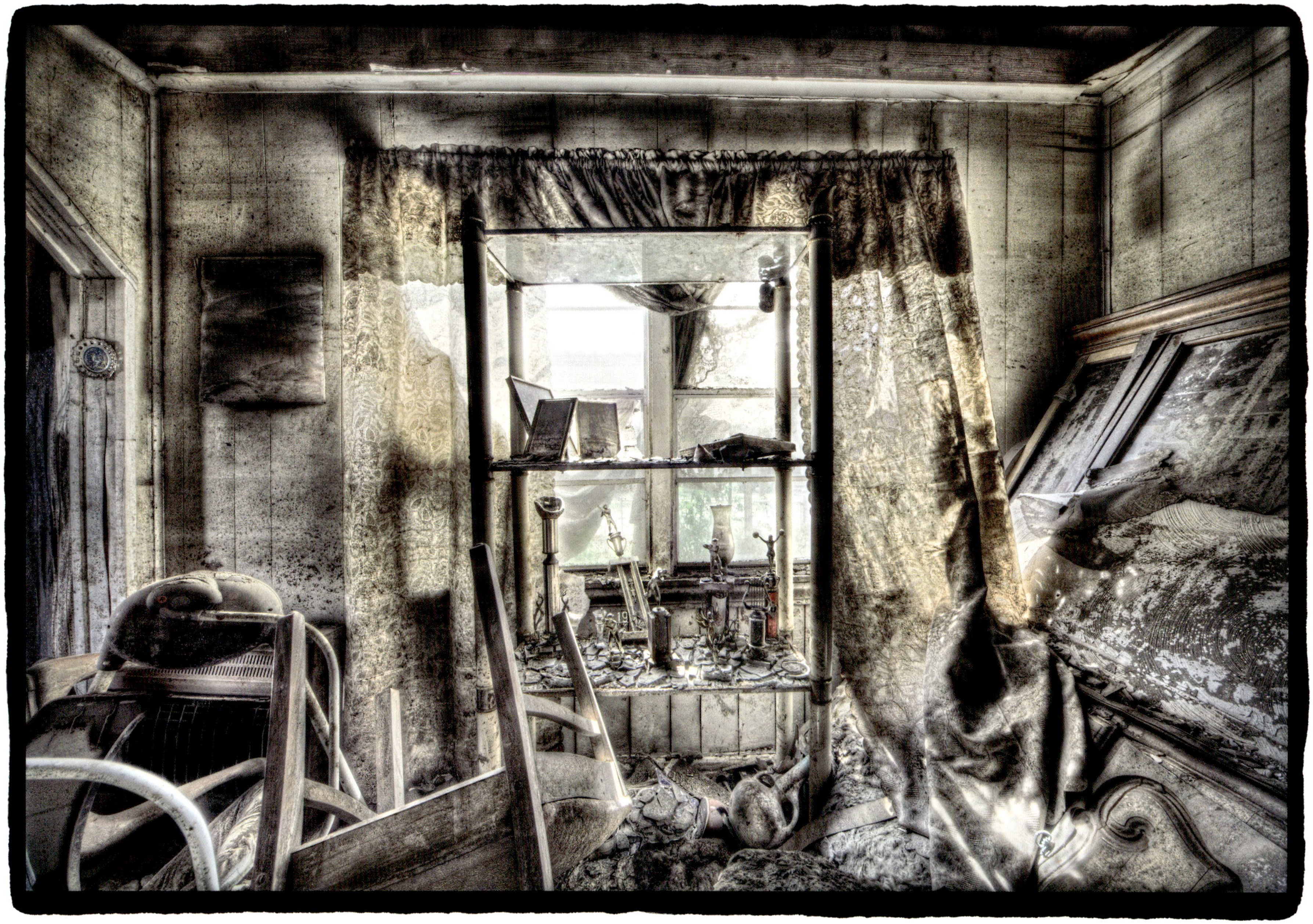

Trophies in Window

Bathroom near Levee

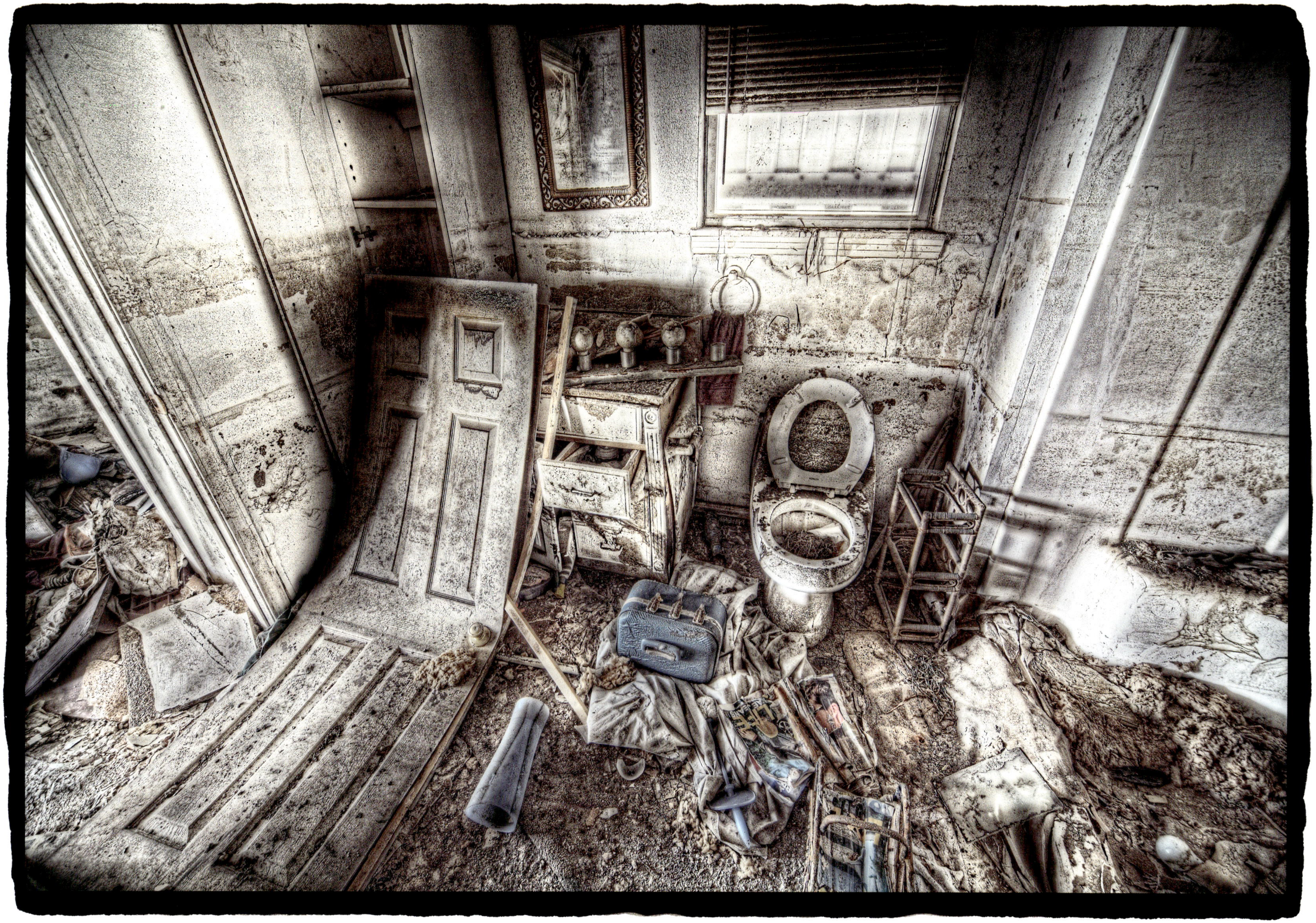

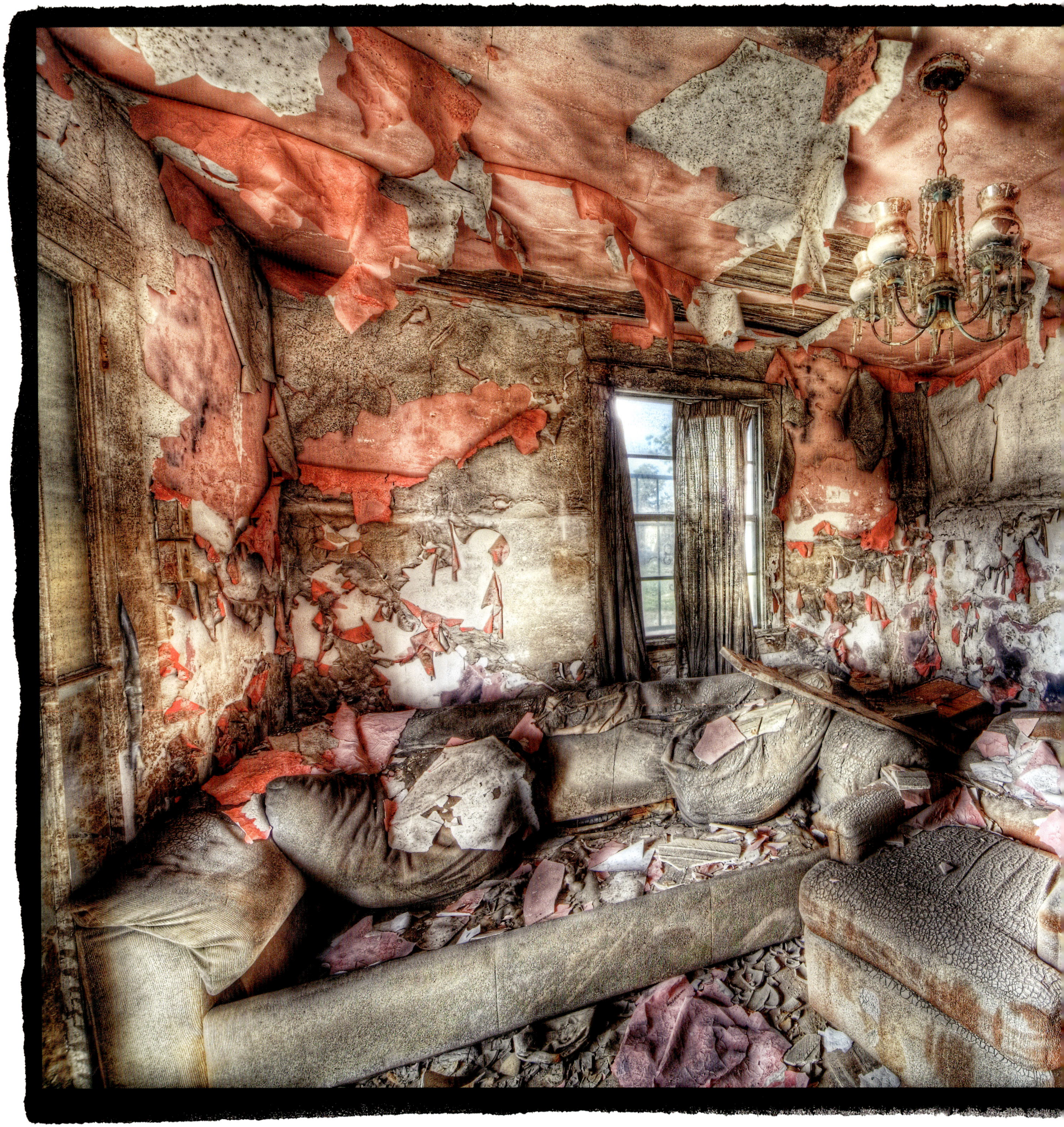

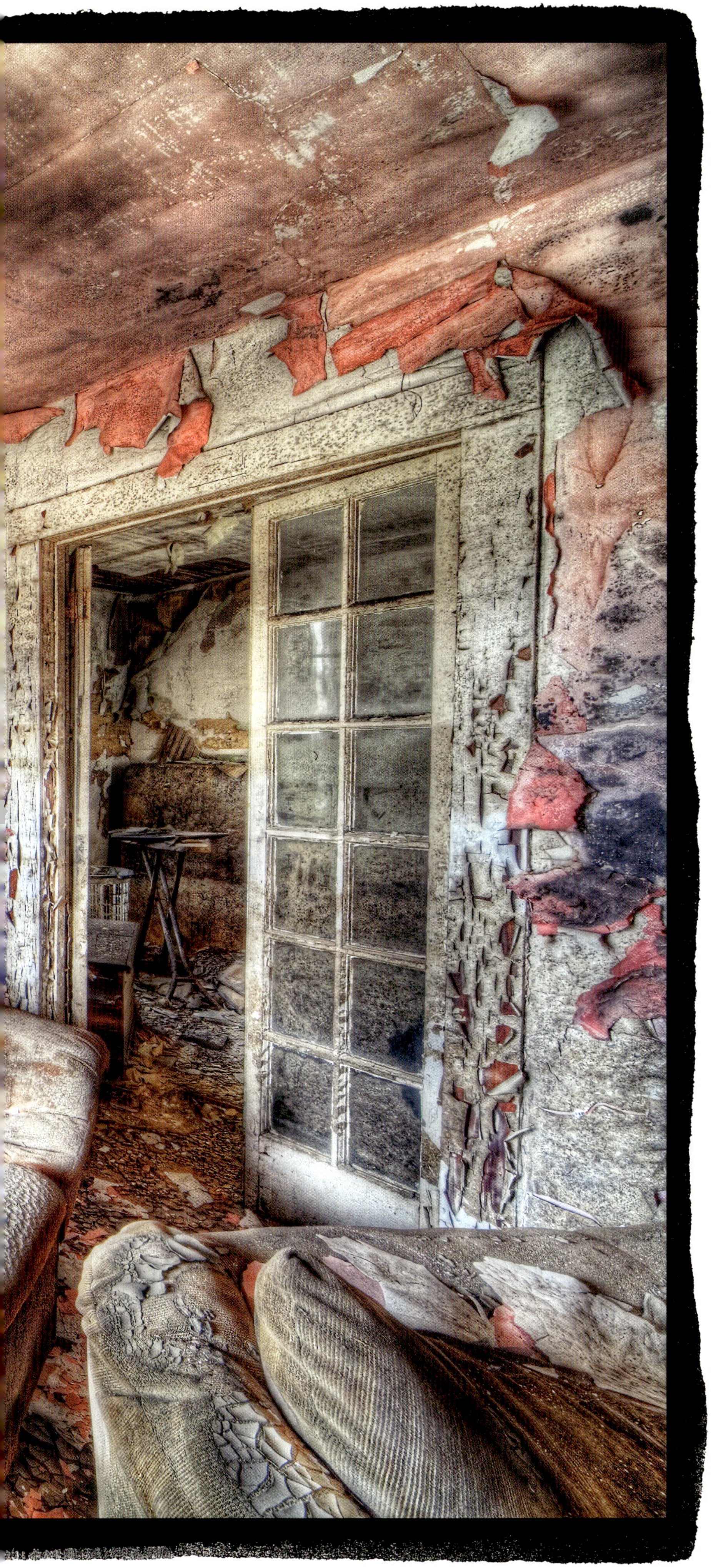

Pink Living Room

Couch with Cushions

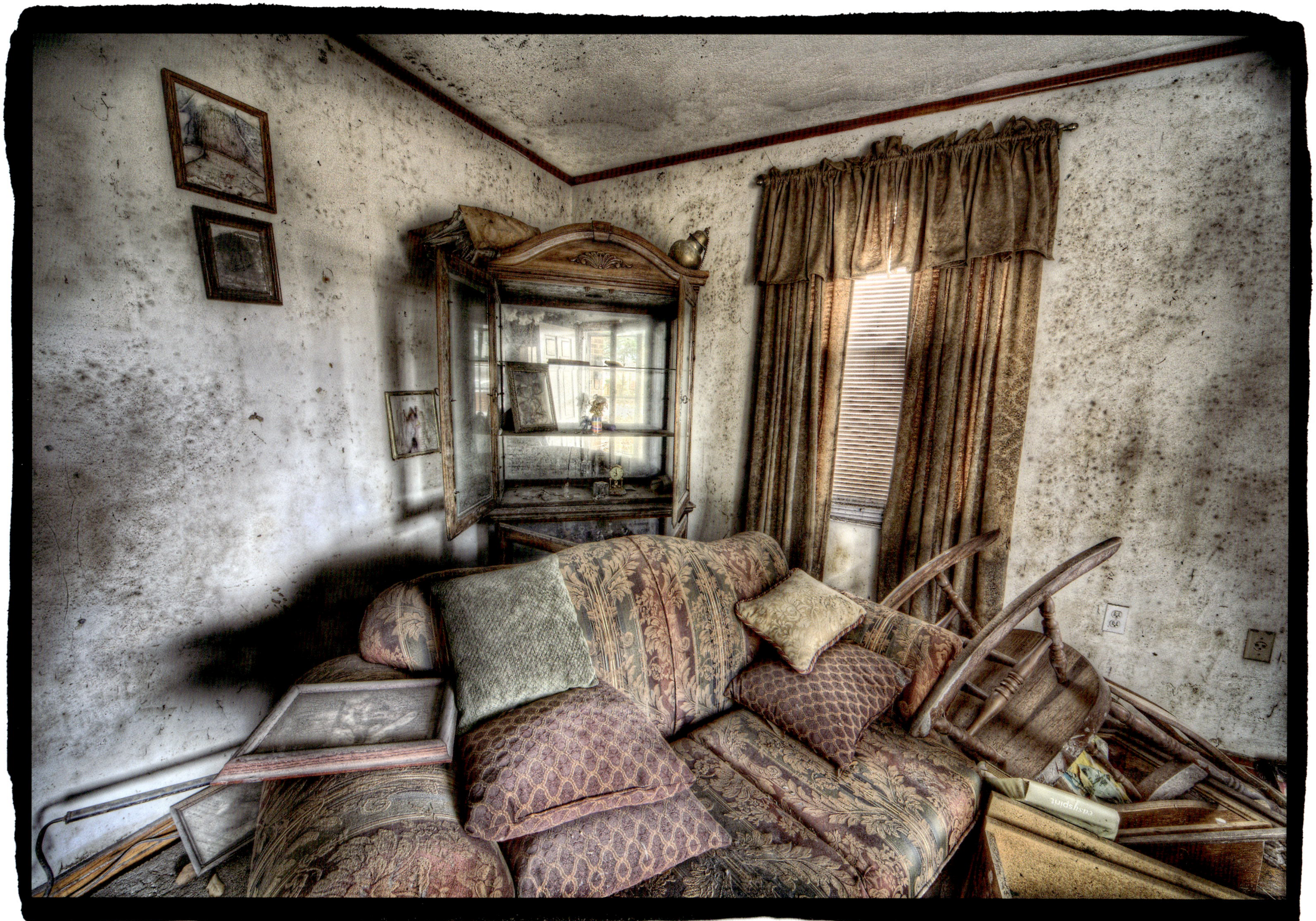

Bookshelf Up Close

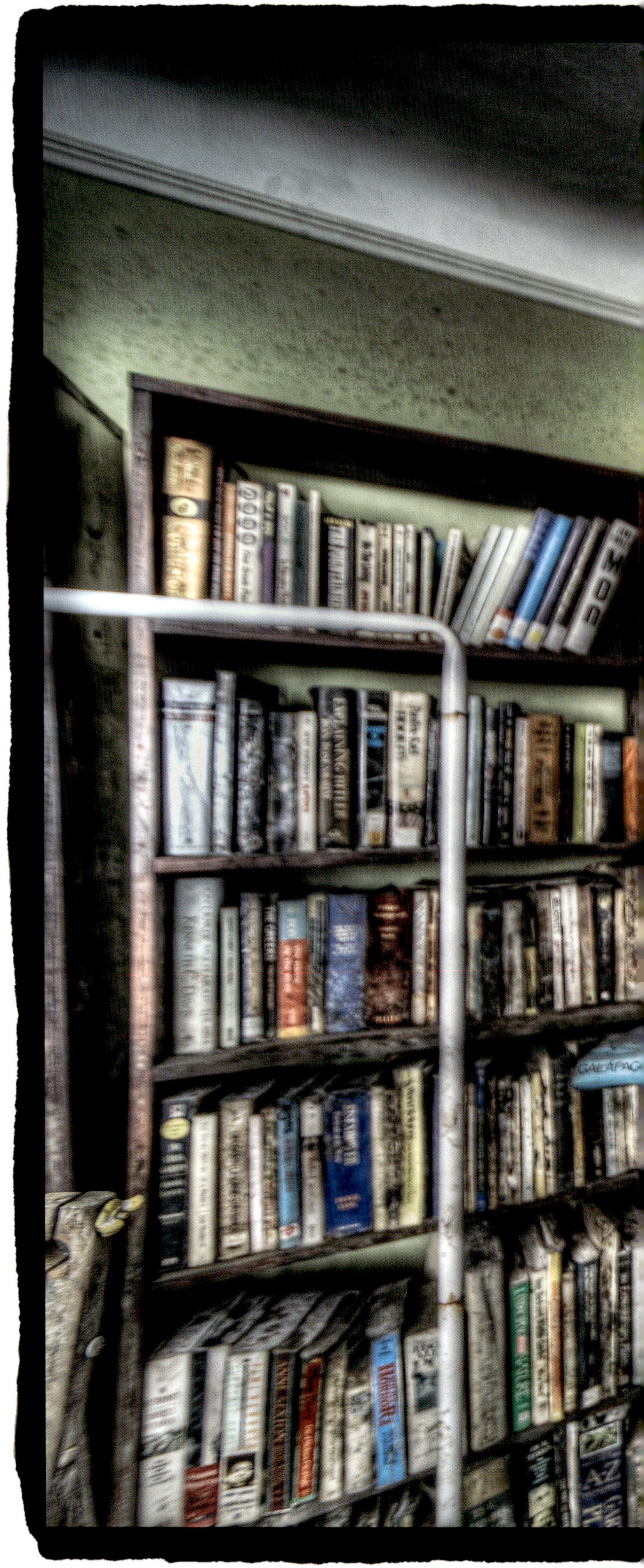

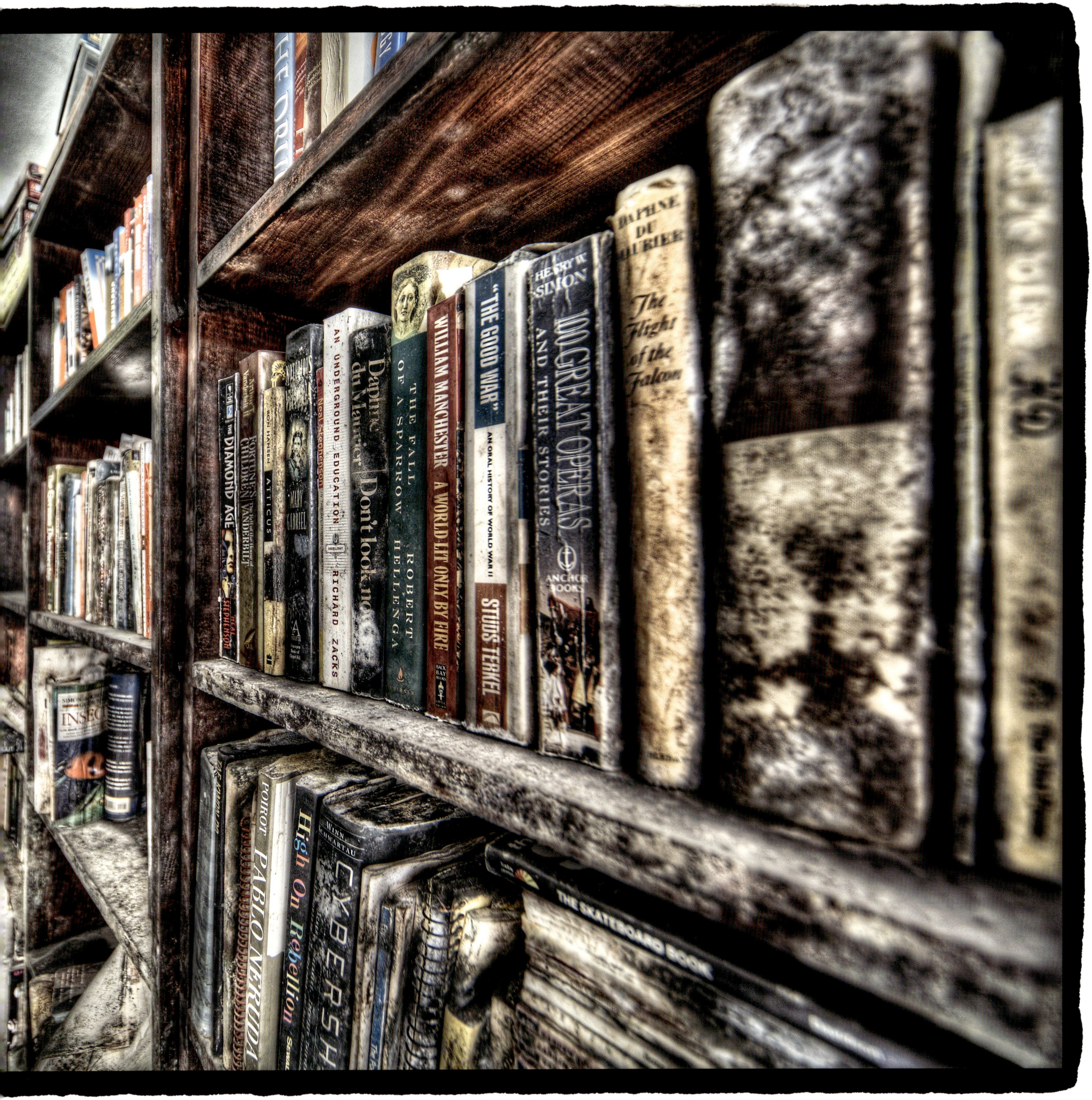
DIAMOND AGE
FORTUNE'S CHILDREN
VANDERBILT
ATTICUS
AN UNDERGROUND EDUCATION
RICHARD ZACKS
Daphne du Maurier
Don't look now
THE FALL OF A SPARROW
ROBERT HELLENGA
WILLIAM MANCHESTER
A WORLD LIT ONLY BY FIRE
"THE GOOD WAR"
AN ORAL HISTORY OF WORLD WAR II
STUDS TERKEL
HENRY W. SIMON
100 GREAT OPERAS AND THEIR STORIES
ANCHOR BOOKS
DAPHNE DU MAURIER
The Flight of the Falcon
PABLO NERUDA
High On Rebellion
THE SKATEBOARD BOOK

Bathroom with Shower Curtain

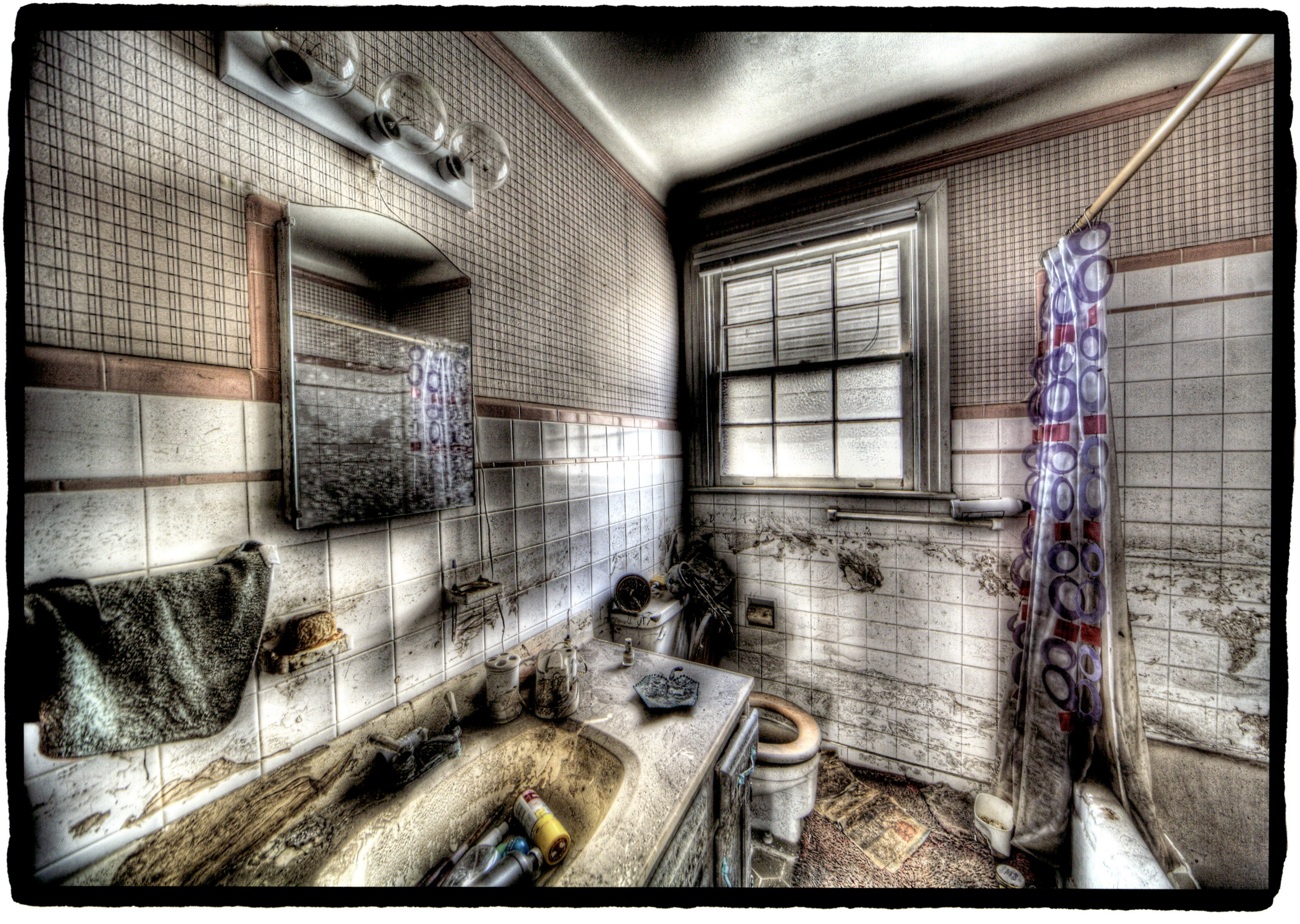

Computer and Window

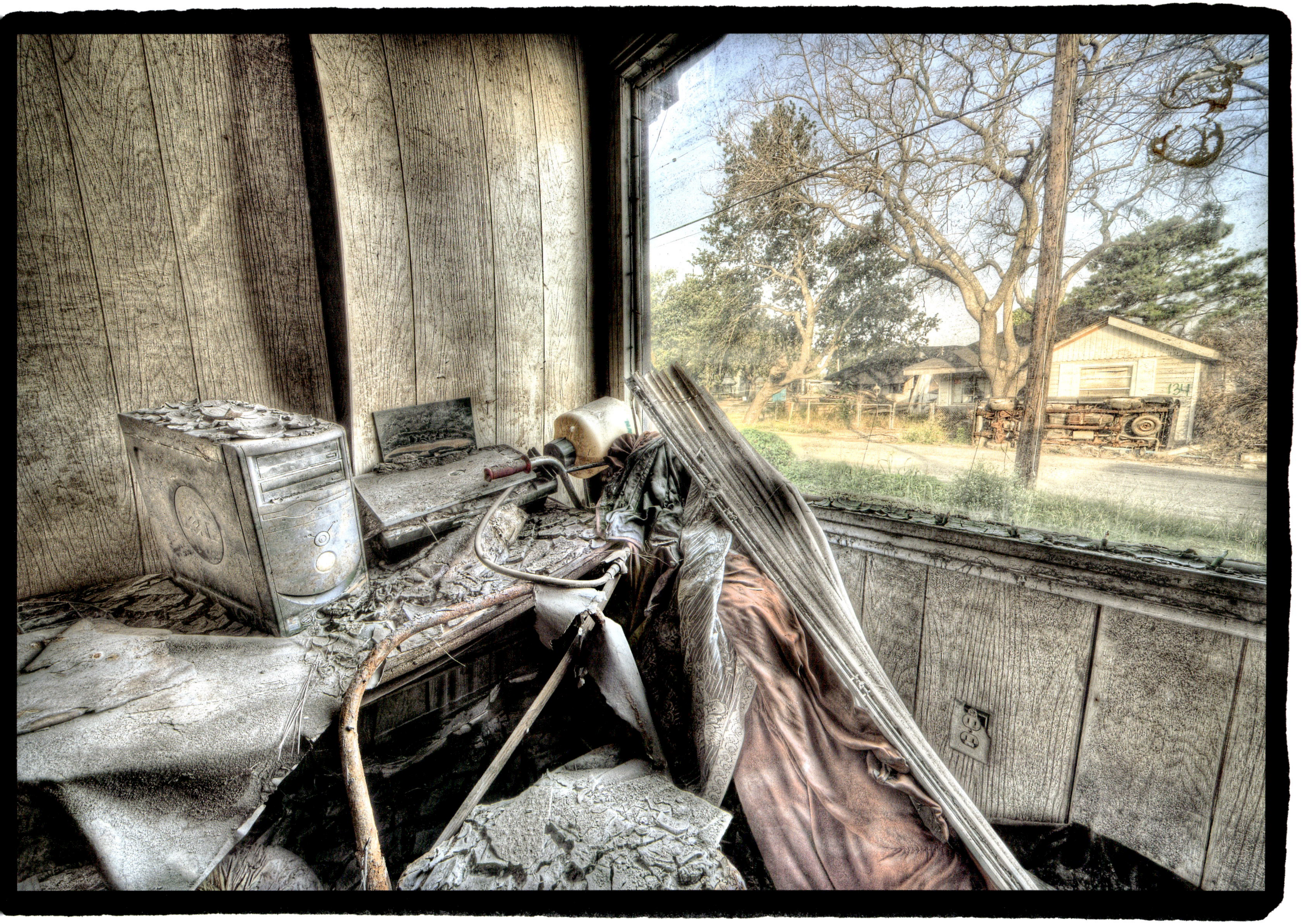
134

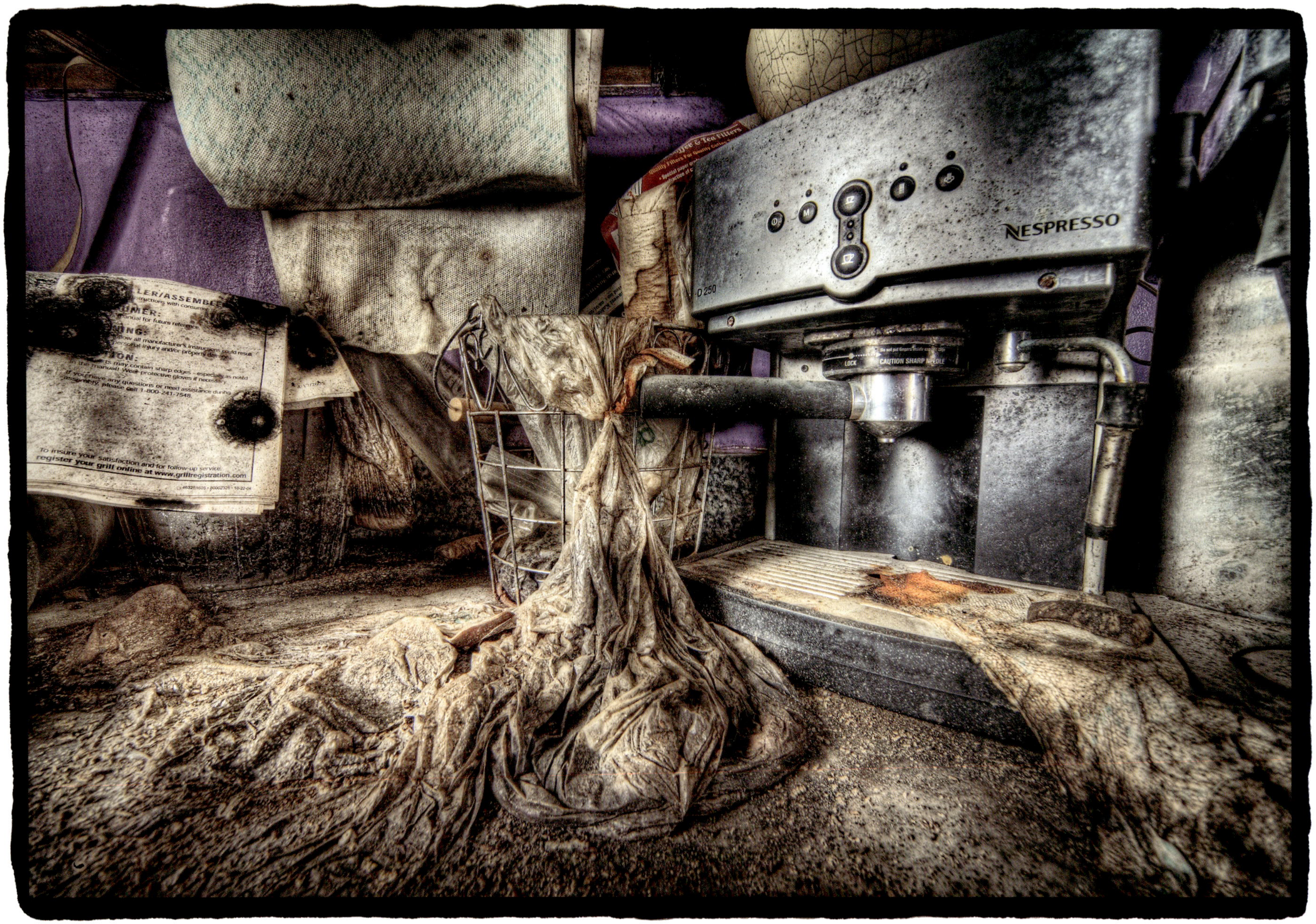

Espresso Machine

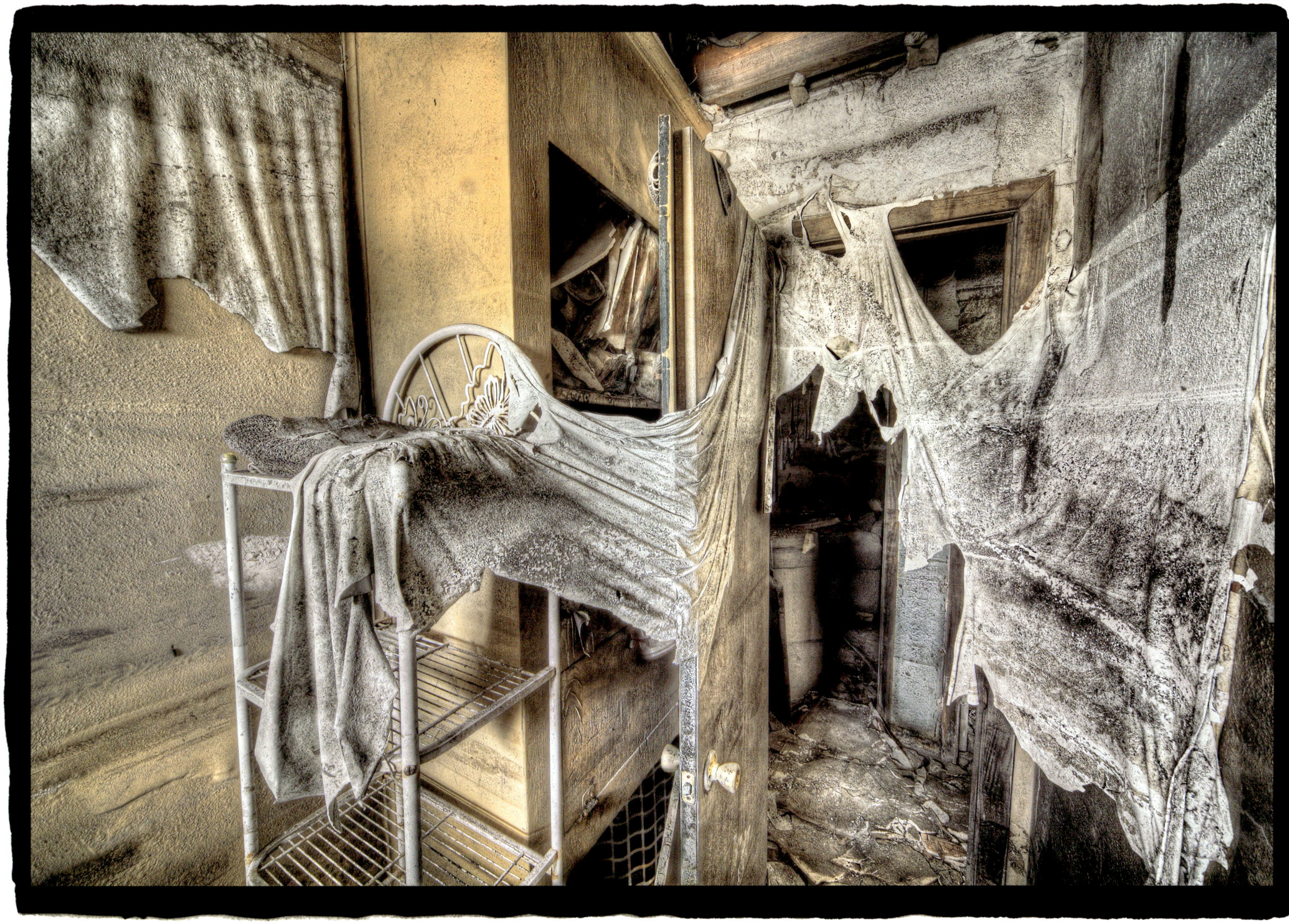

Drooping Paint

Clothes in Green Room

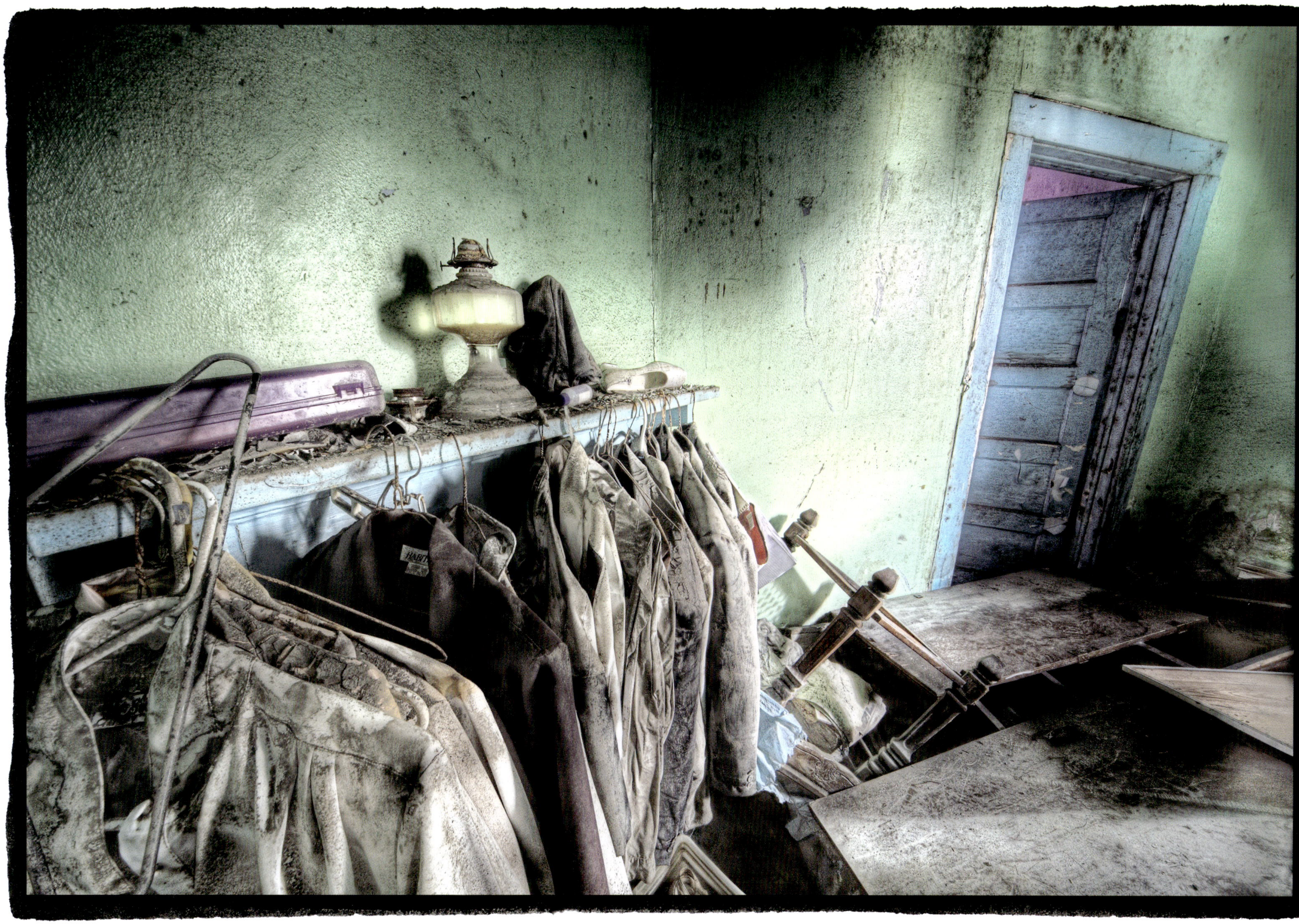

Housedress in Bedroom

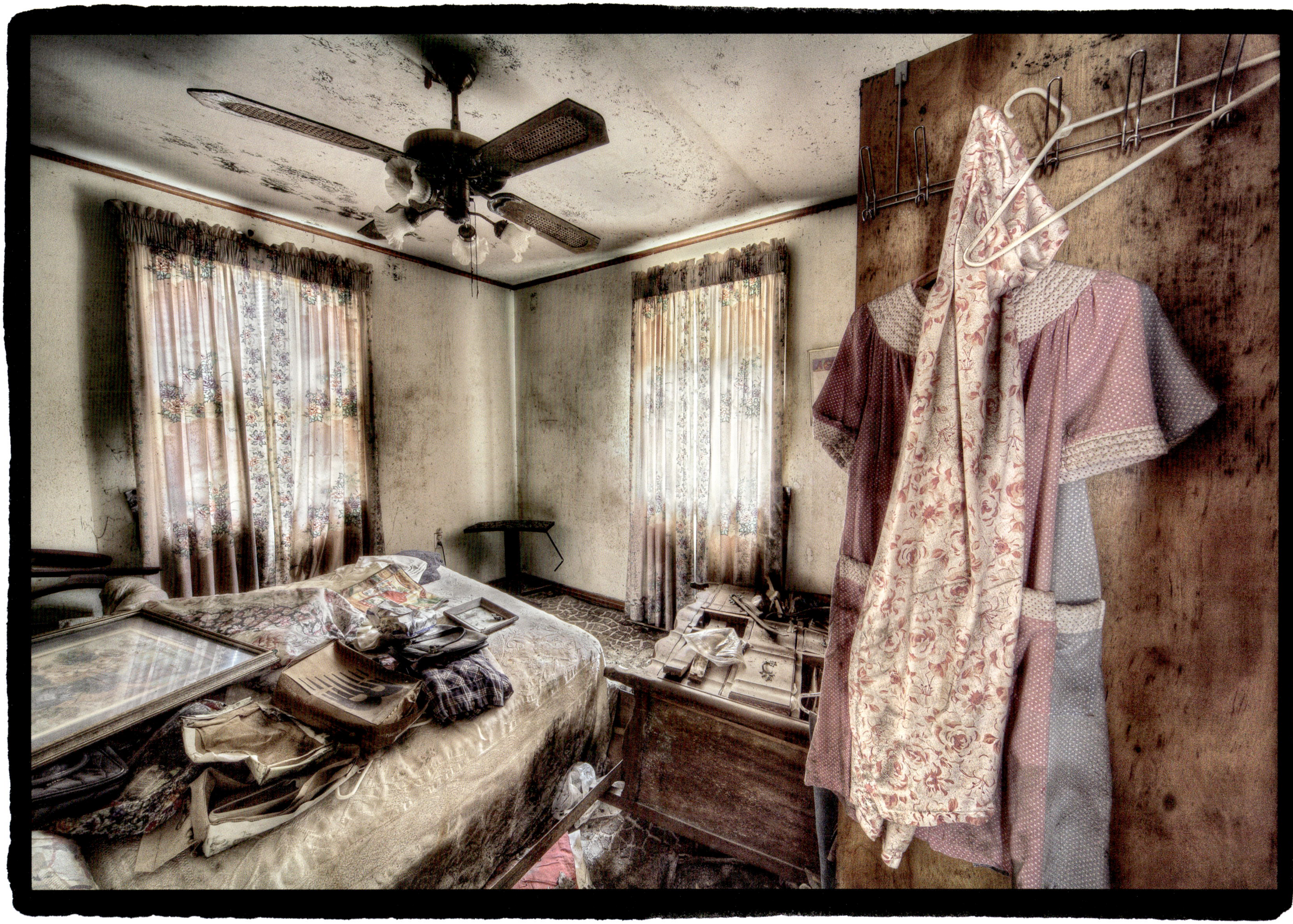

Ironing Board

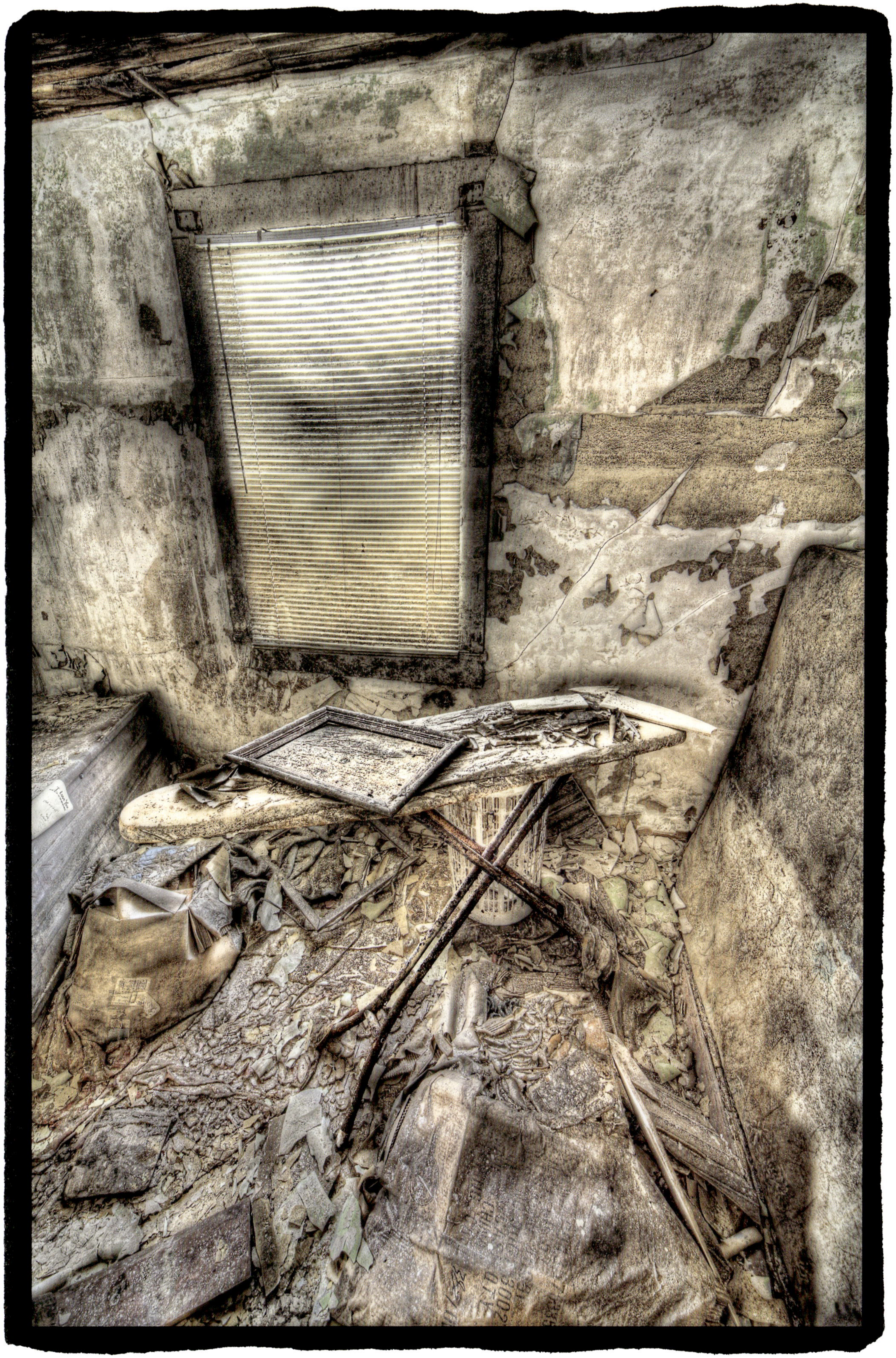

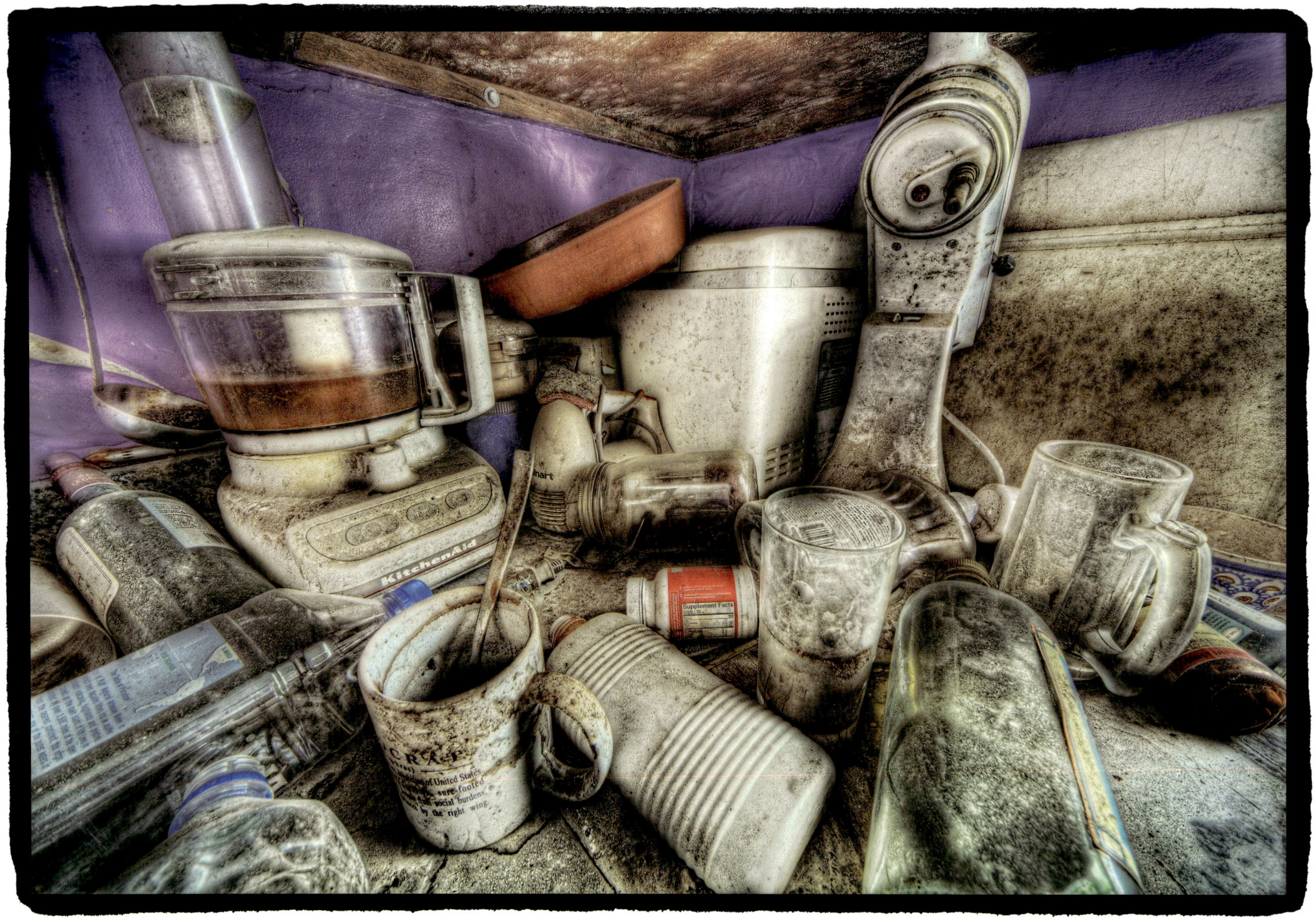

Floodwater in Food Processor

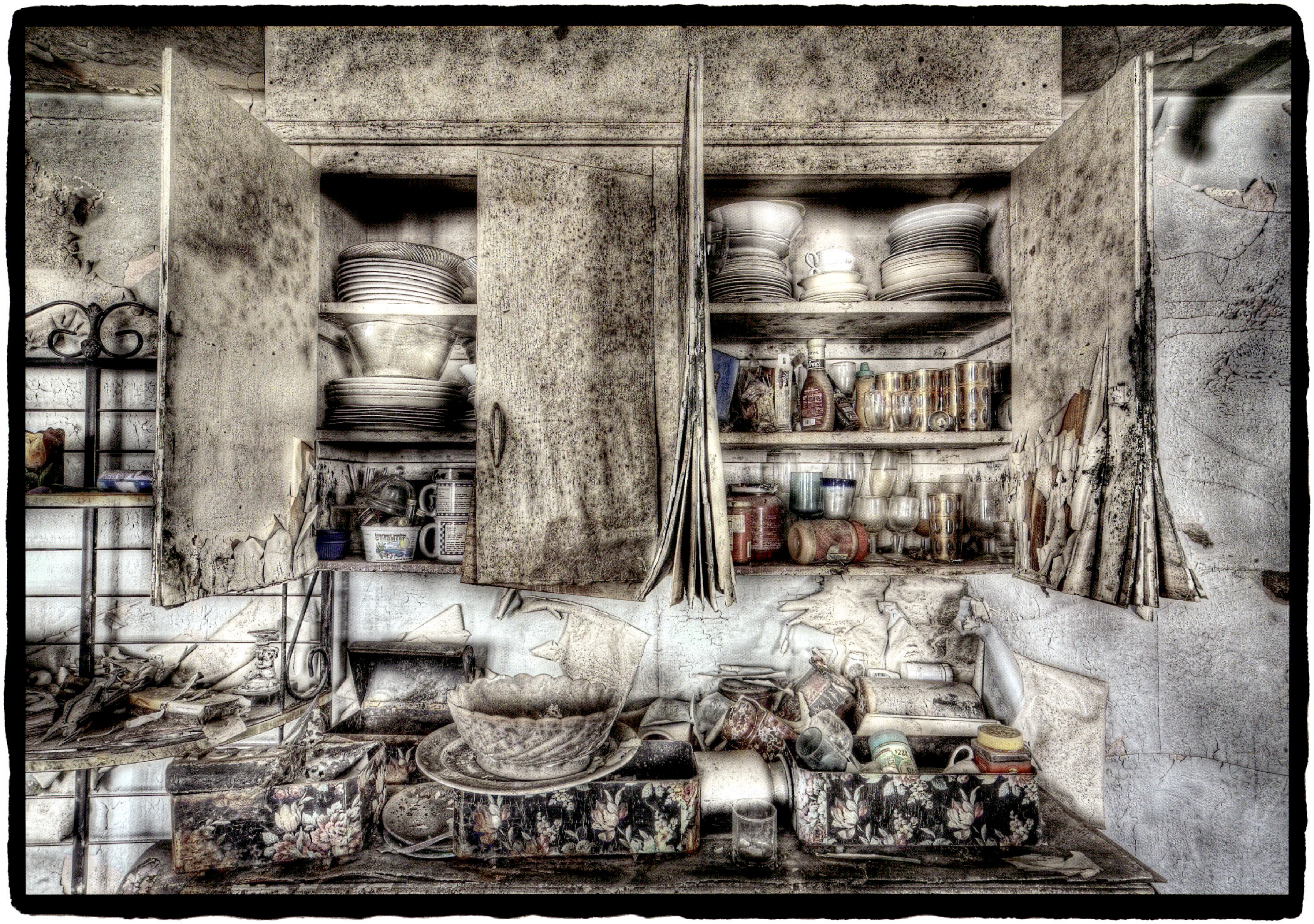

Kitchen Cupboard

Sink and Soap Dish

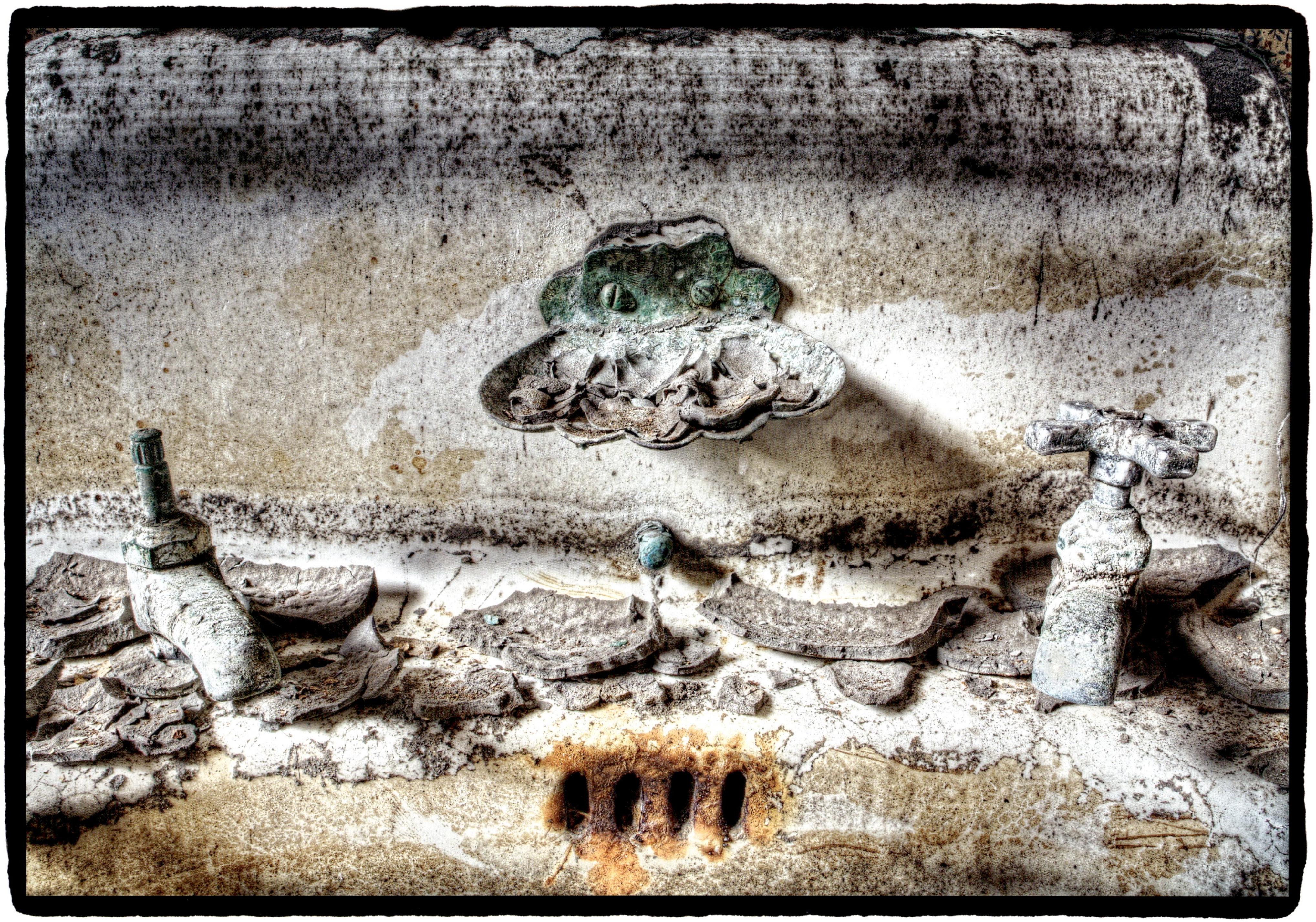

Senior's Bathroom

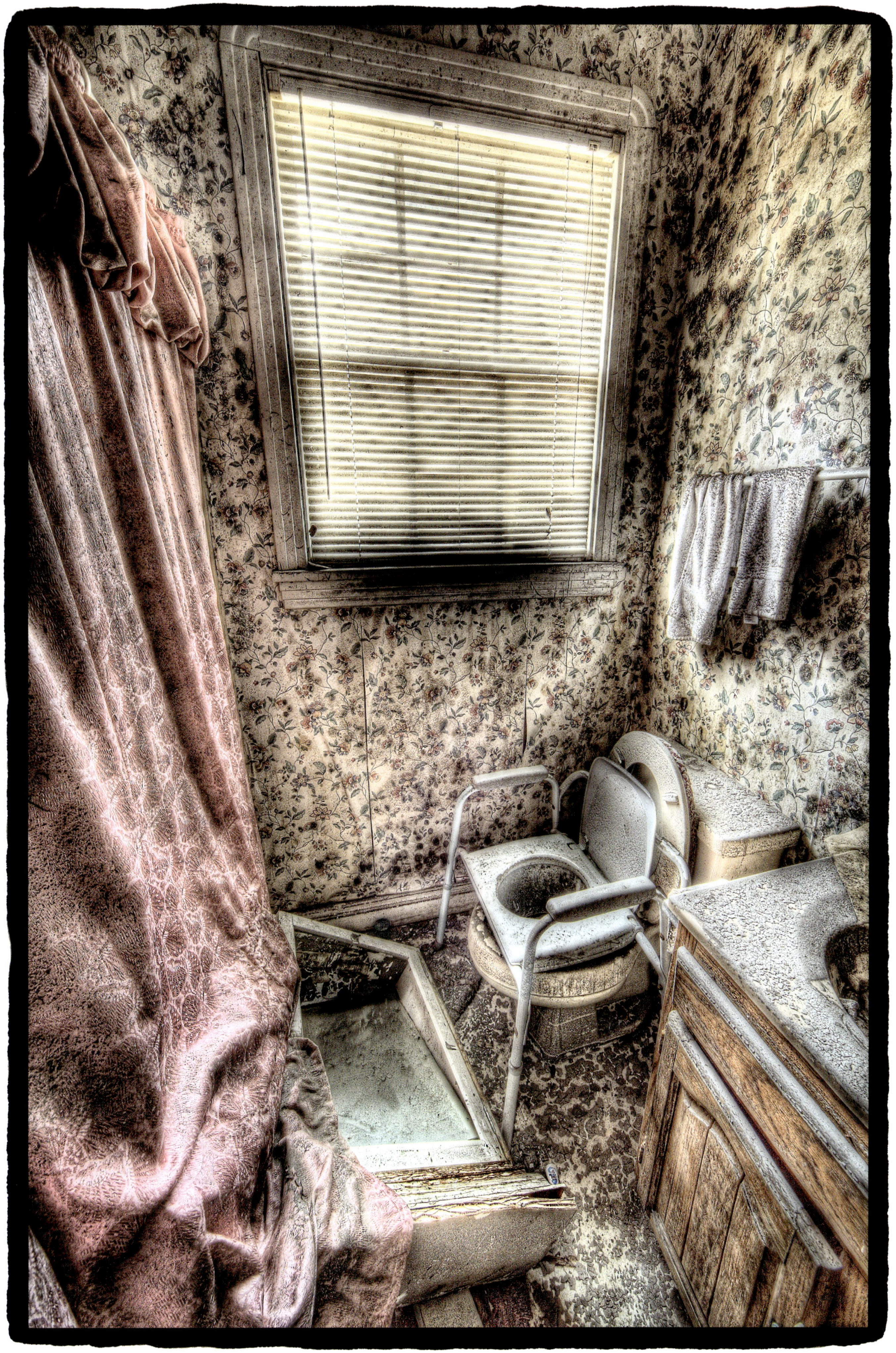

Weight Room

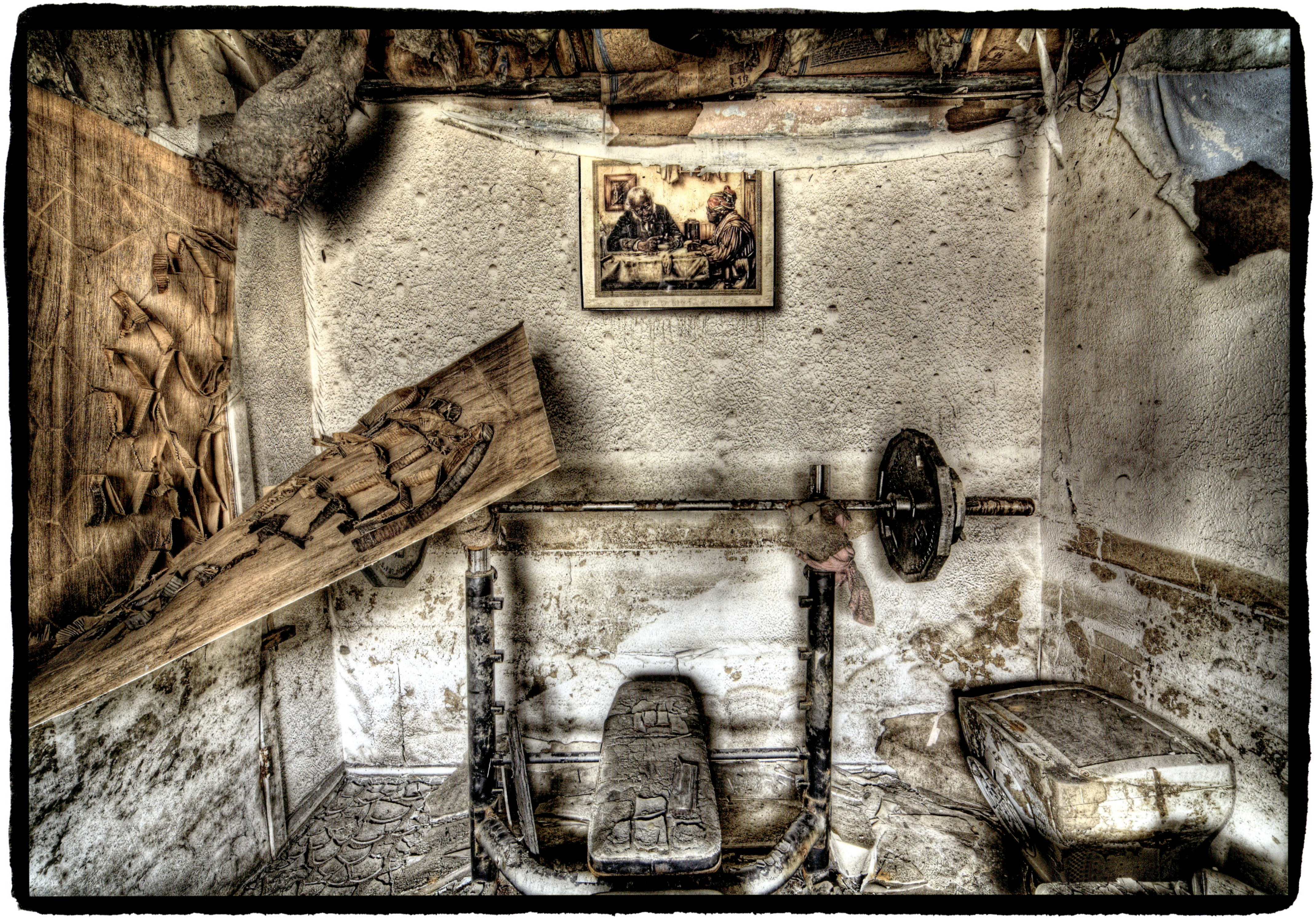

Church with Organ

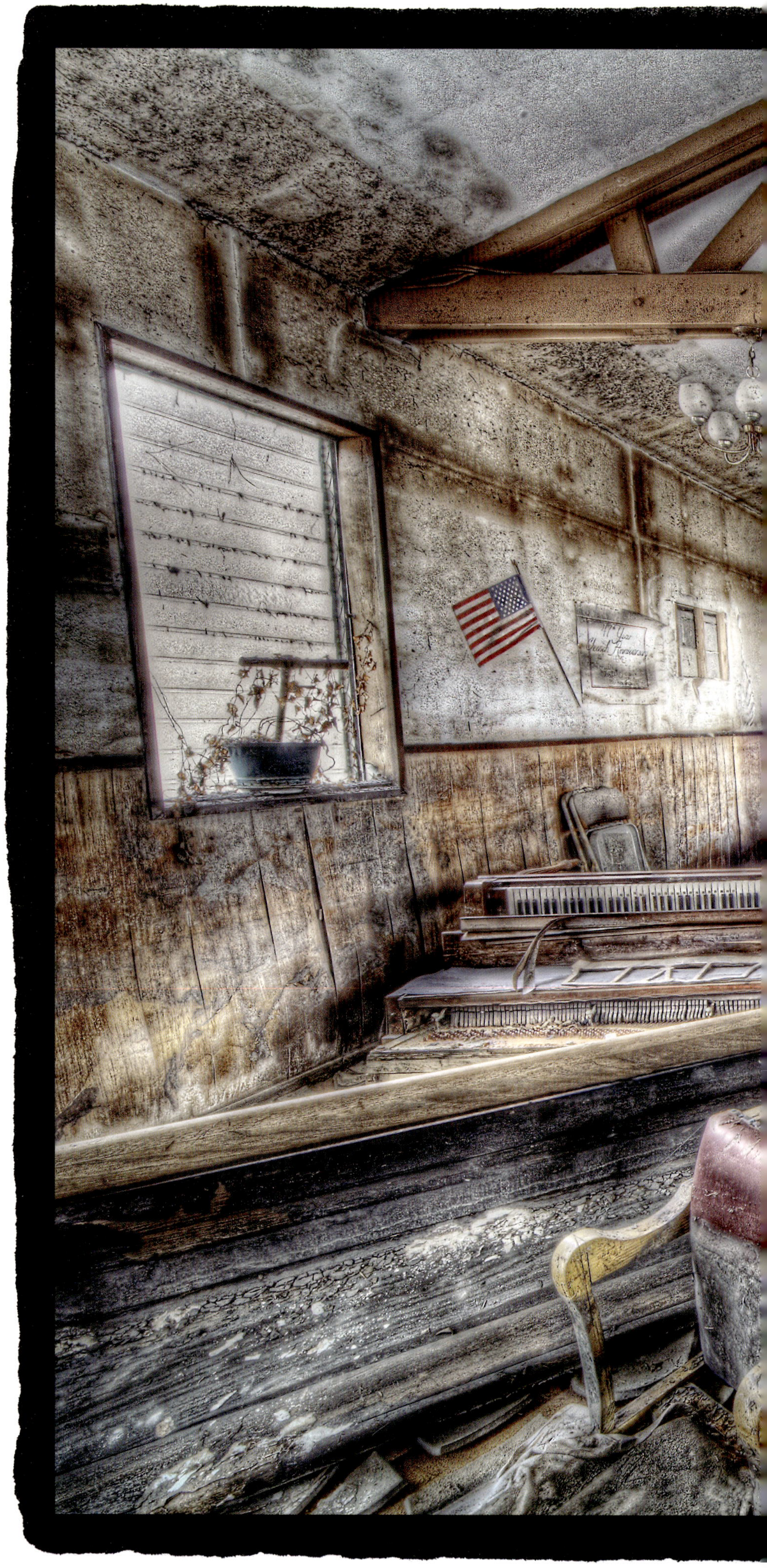

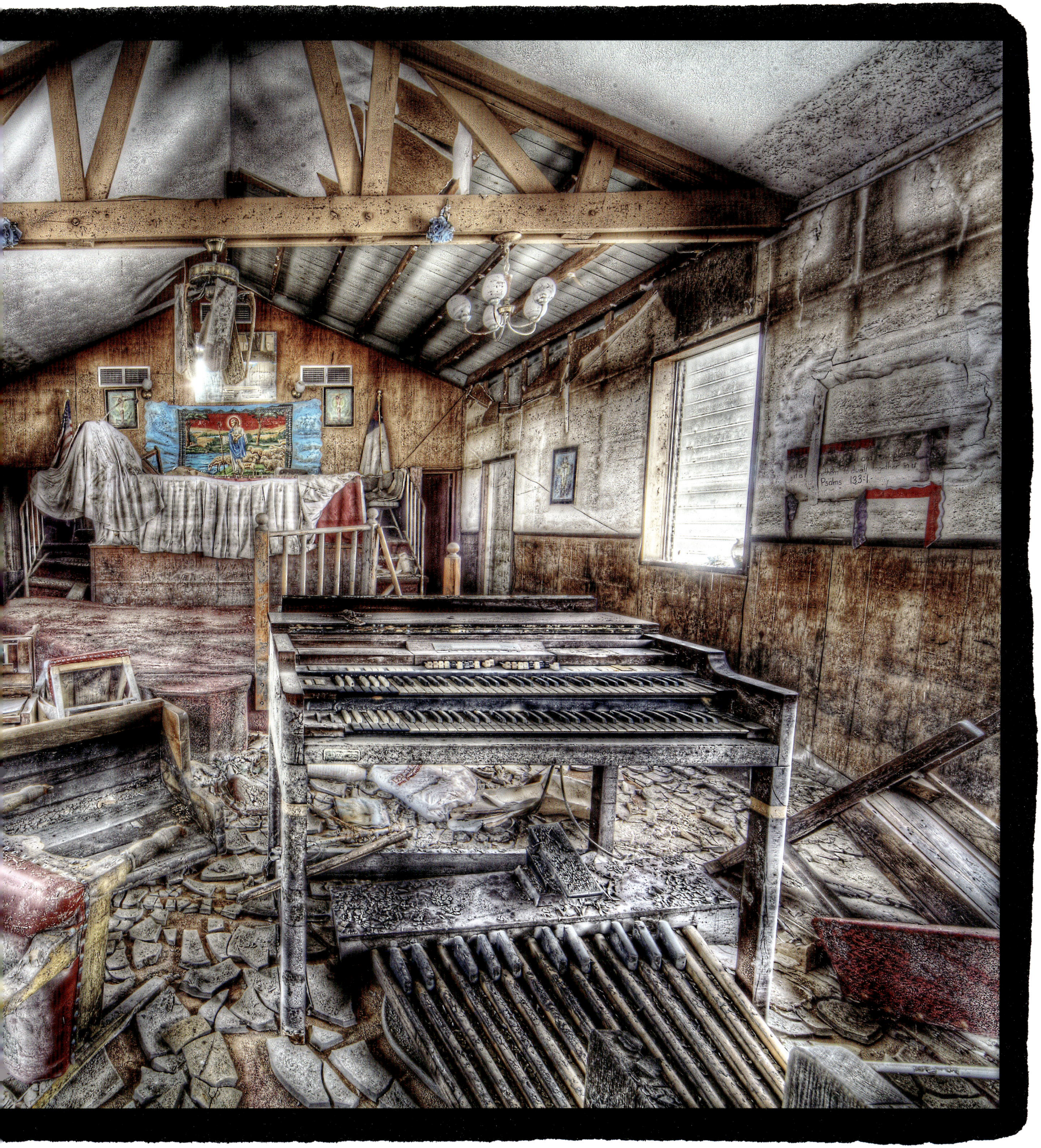
Psalms 133:1

Stained Glass and Chairs

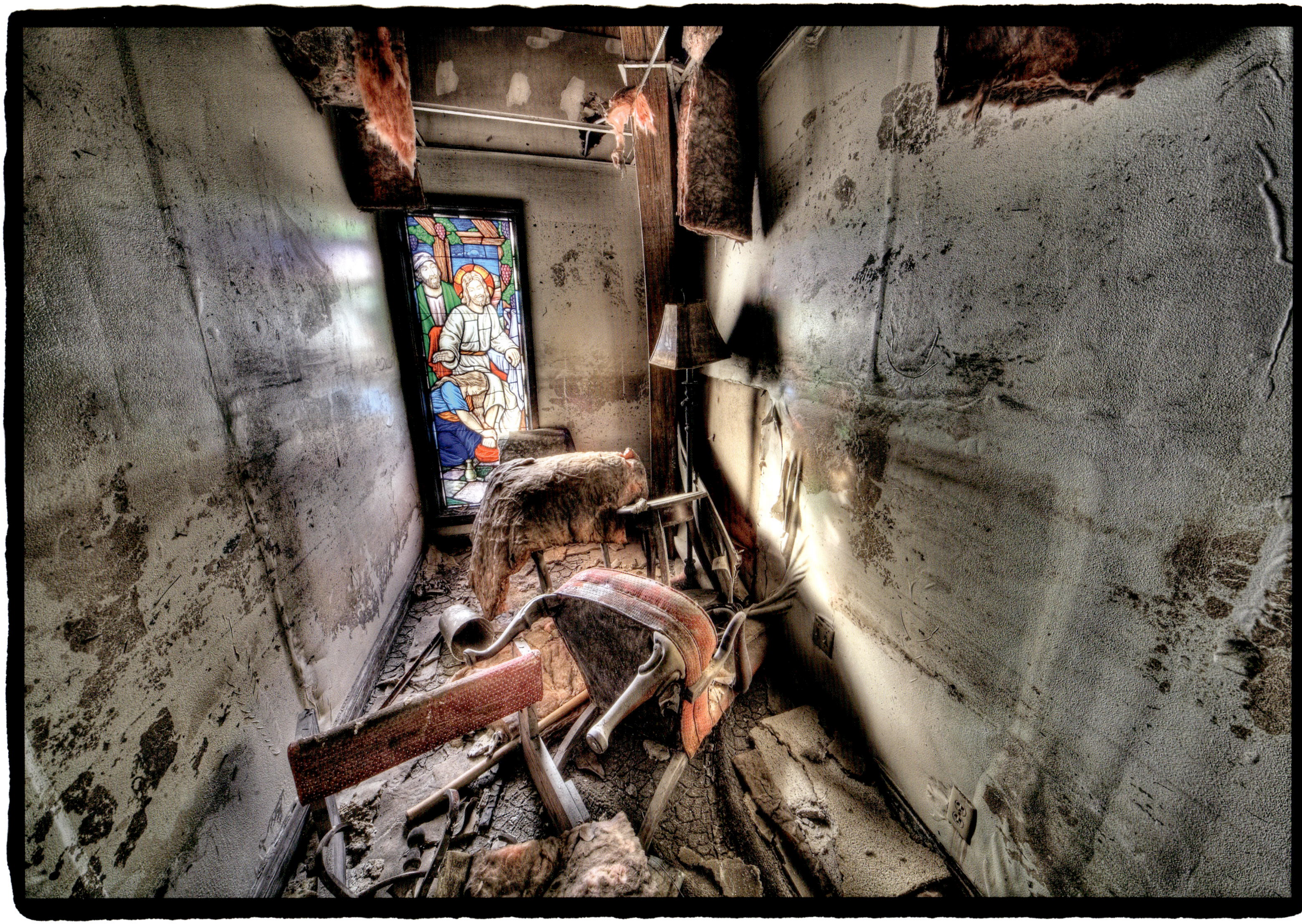

Christ and Candles

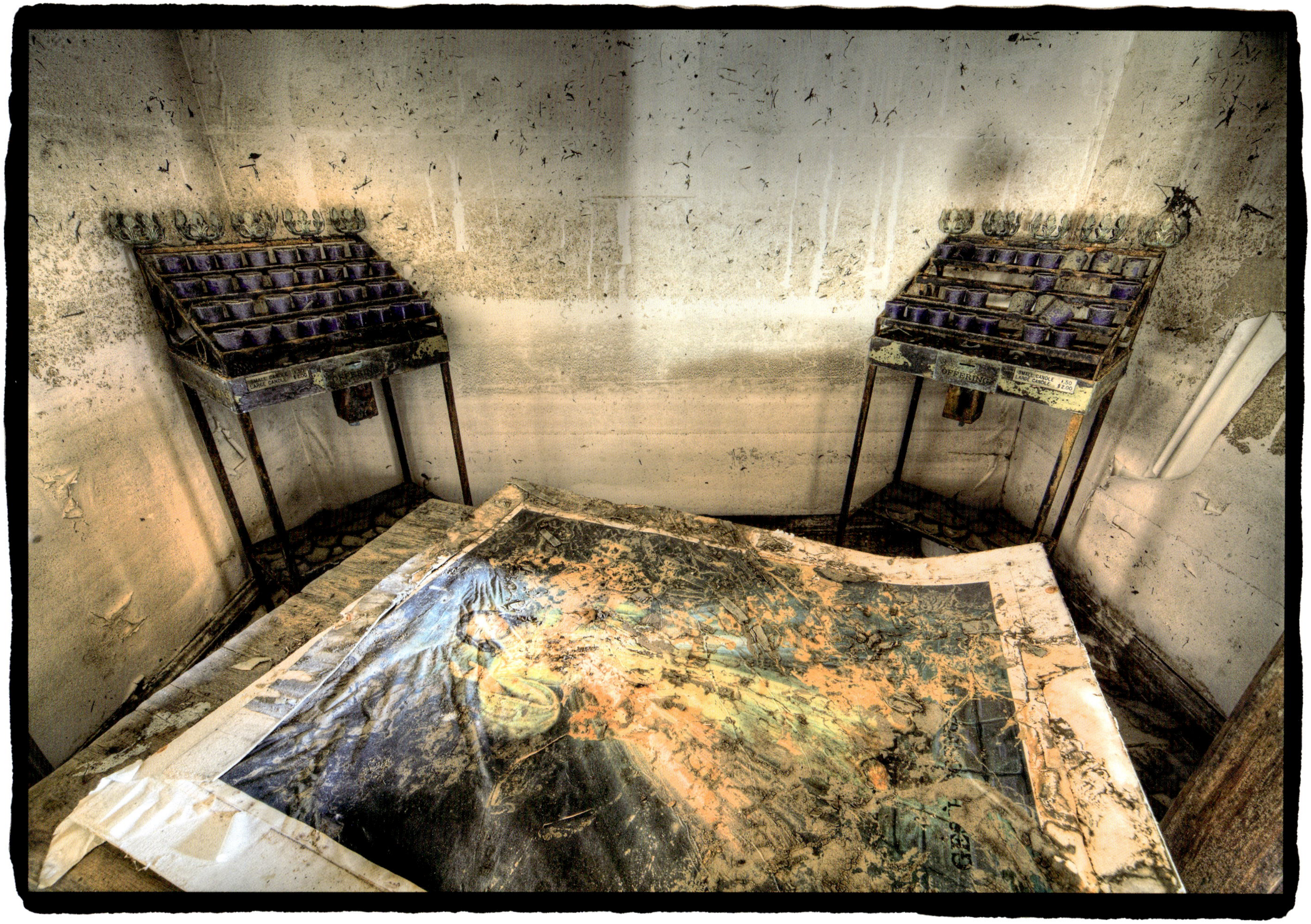
OFFERING
SMALL CANDLE $.50
LARGE CANDLE $2.00

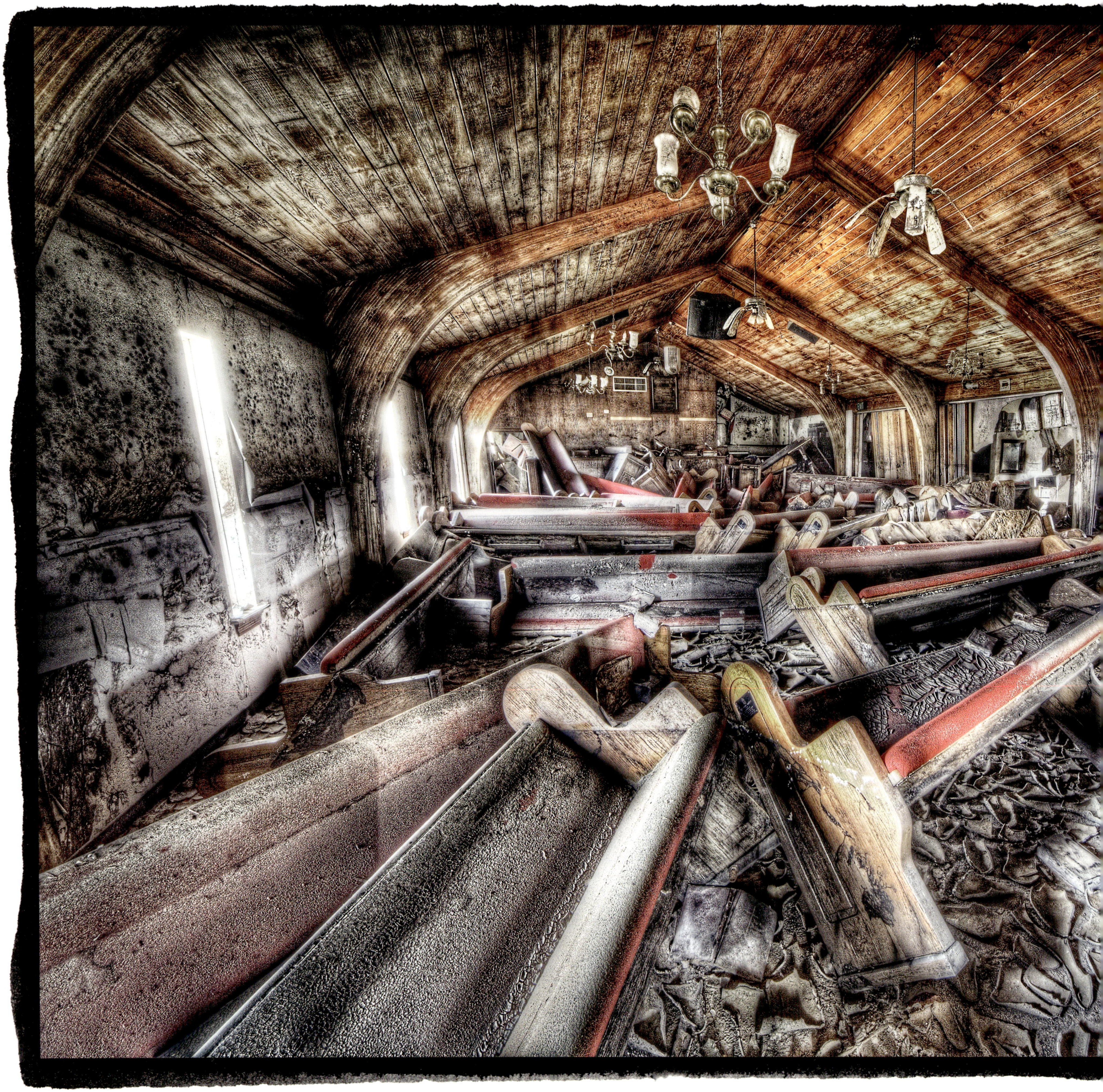

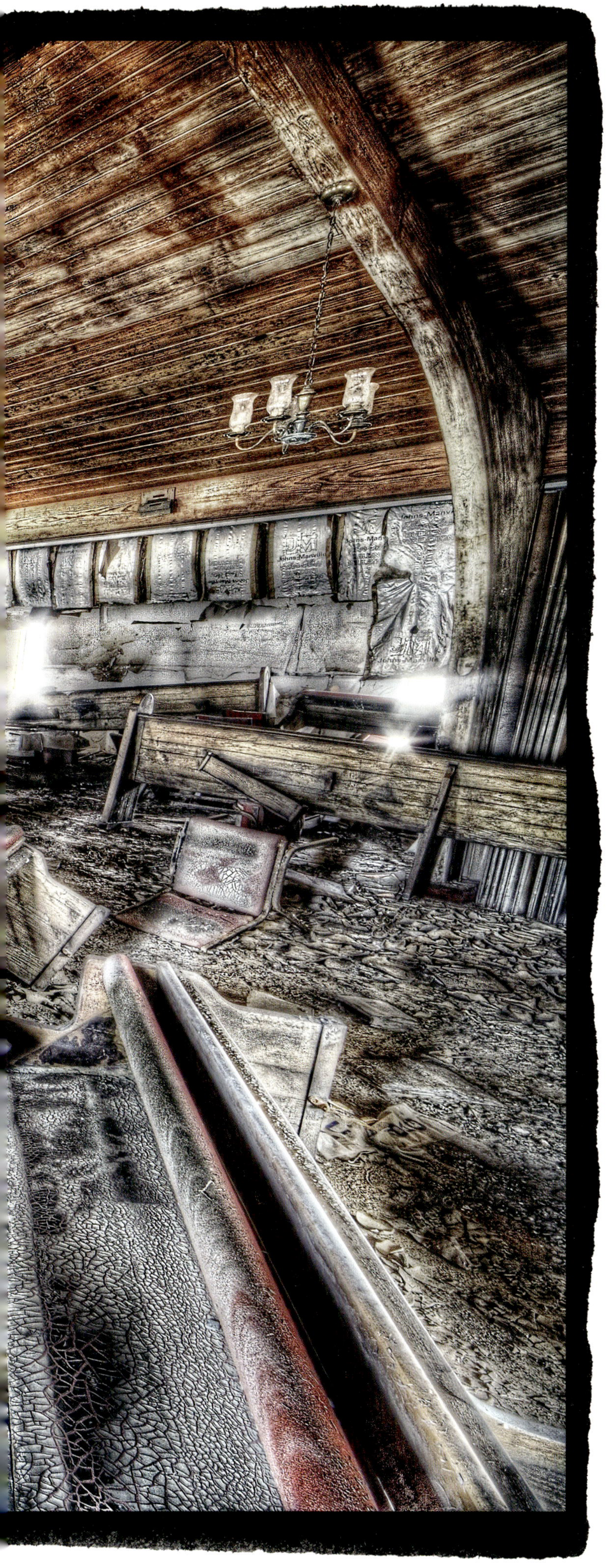

Church Pews

Church Pew in Bathroom

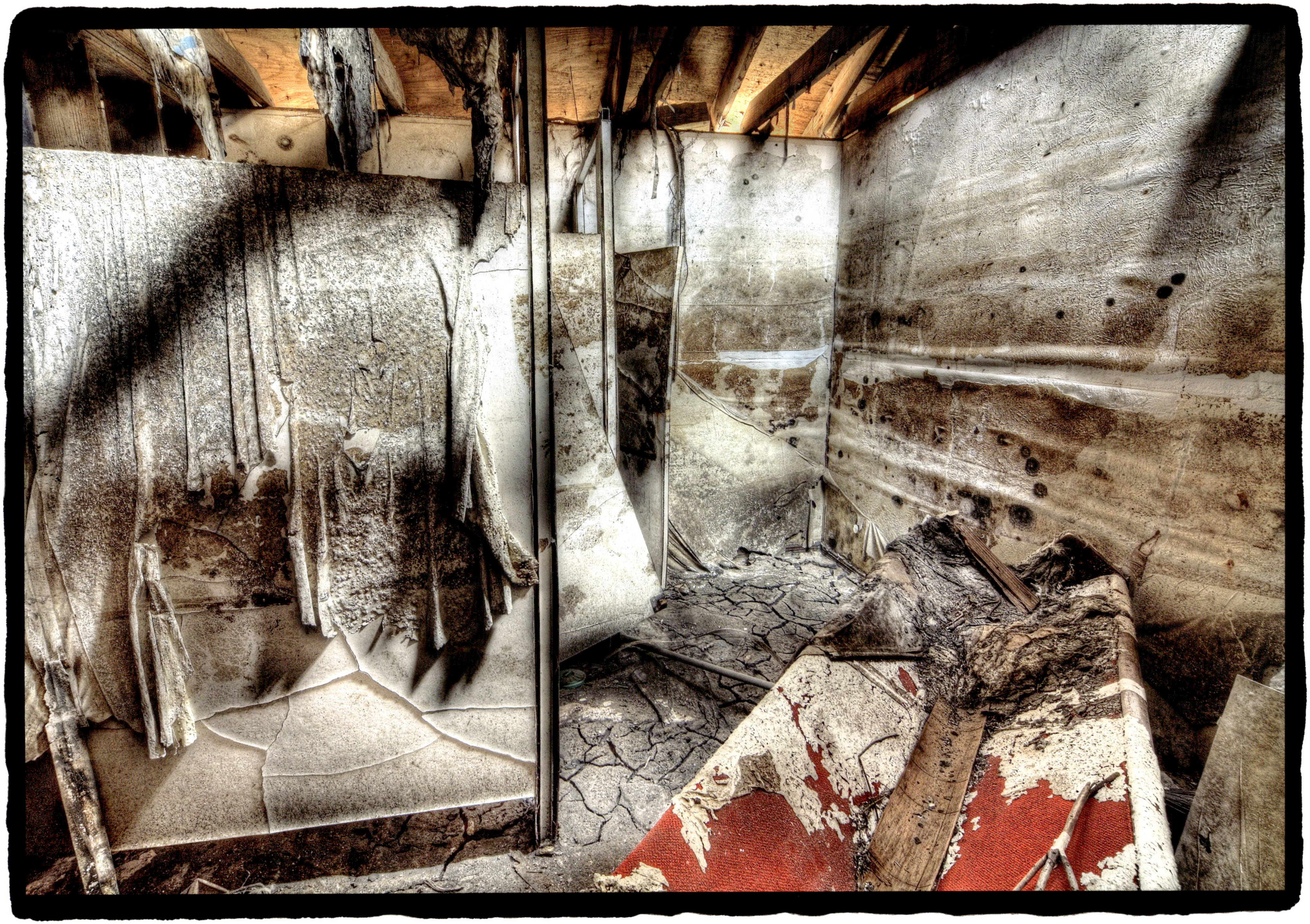

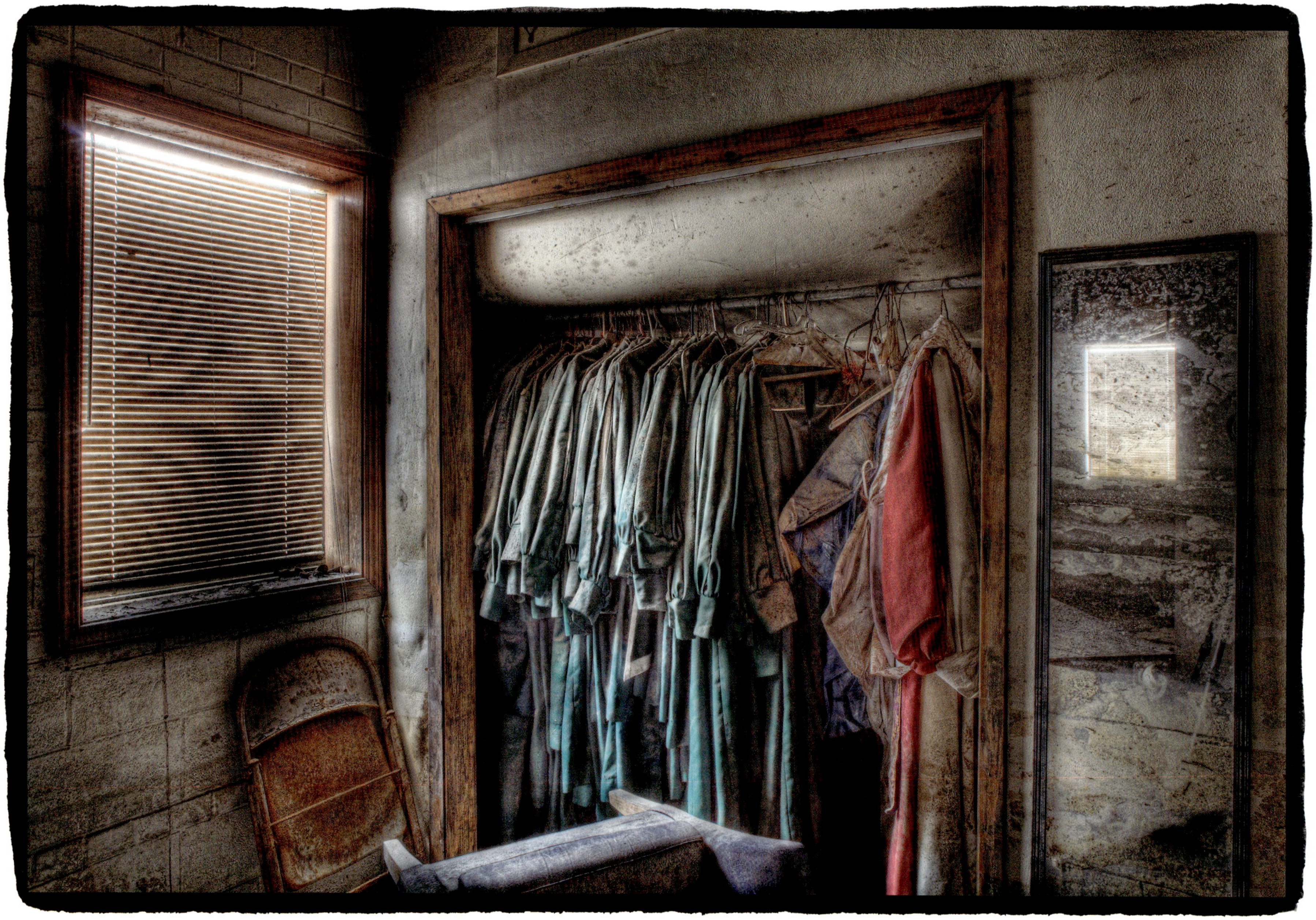

Green Choir Robes

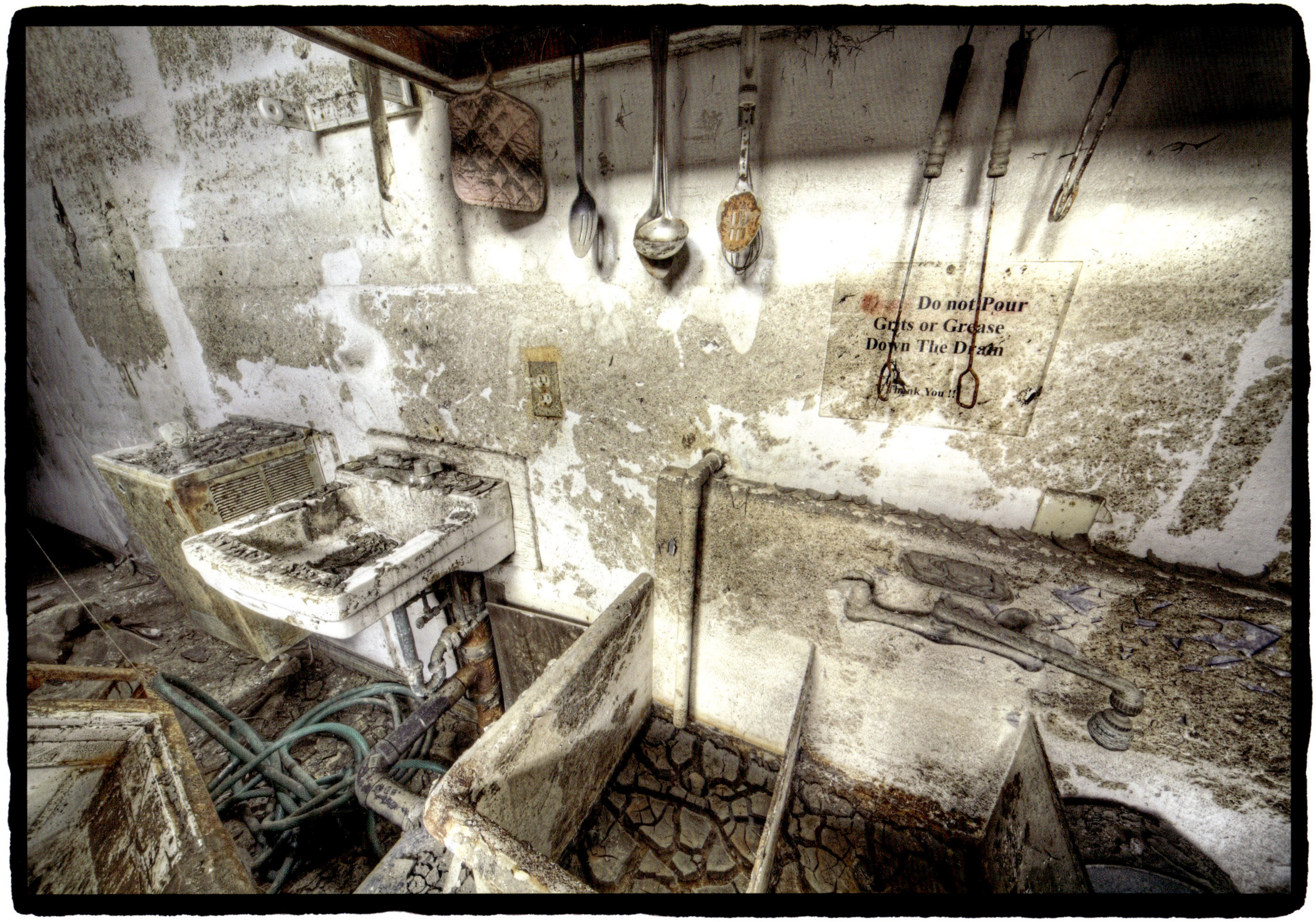

Sign over Church Sink

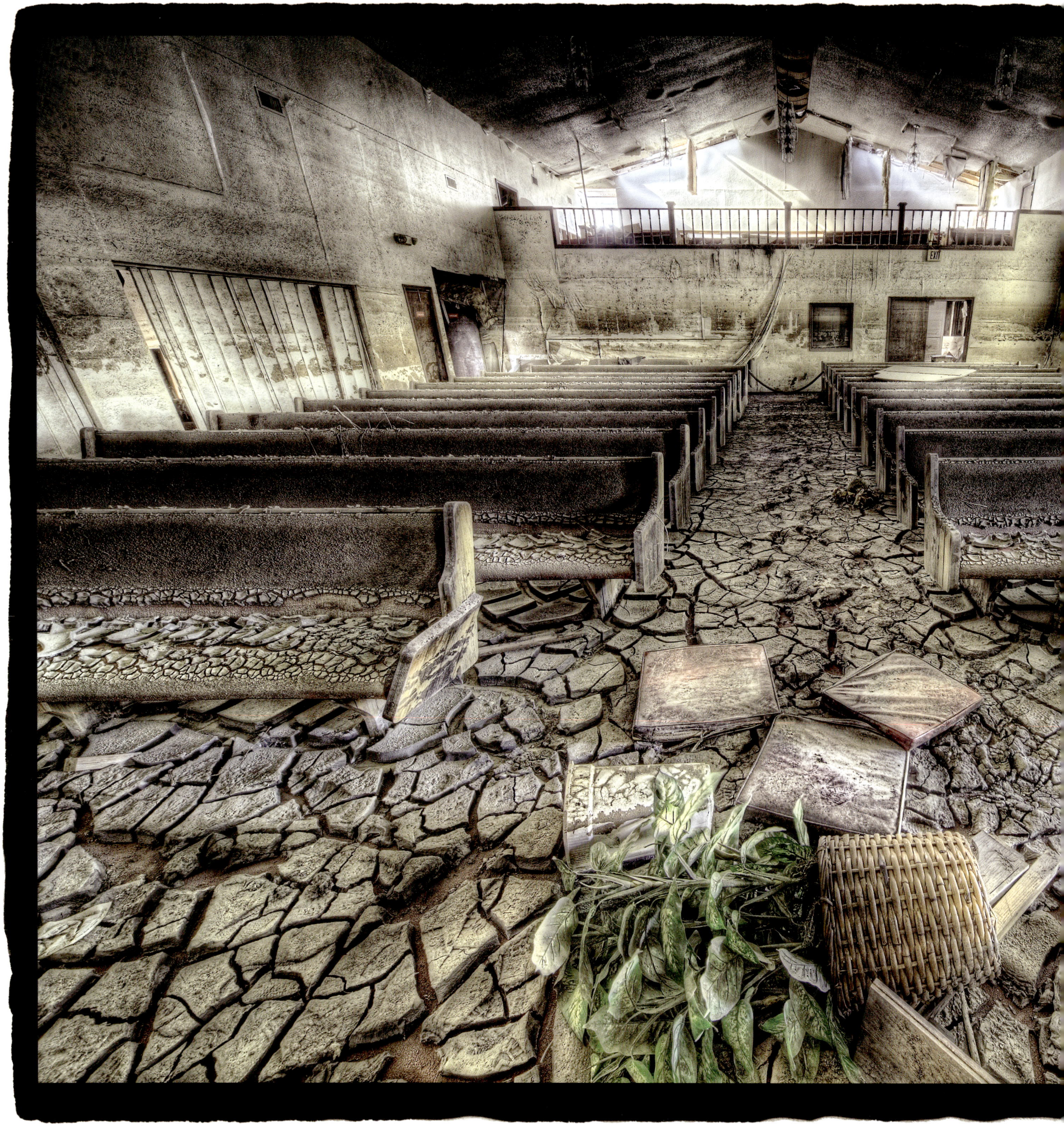

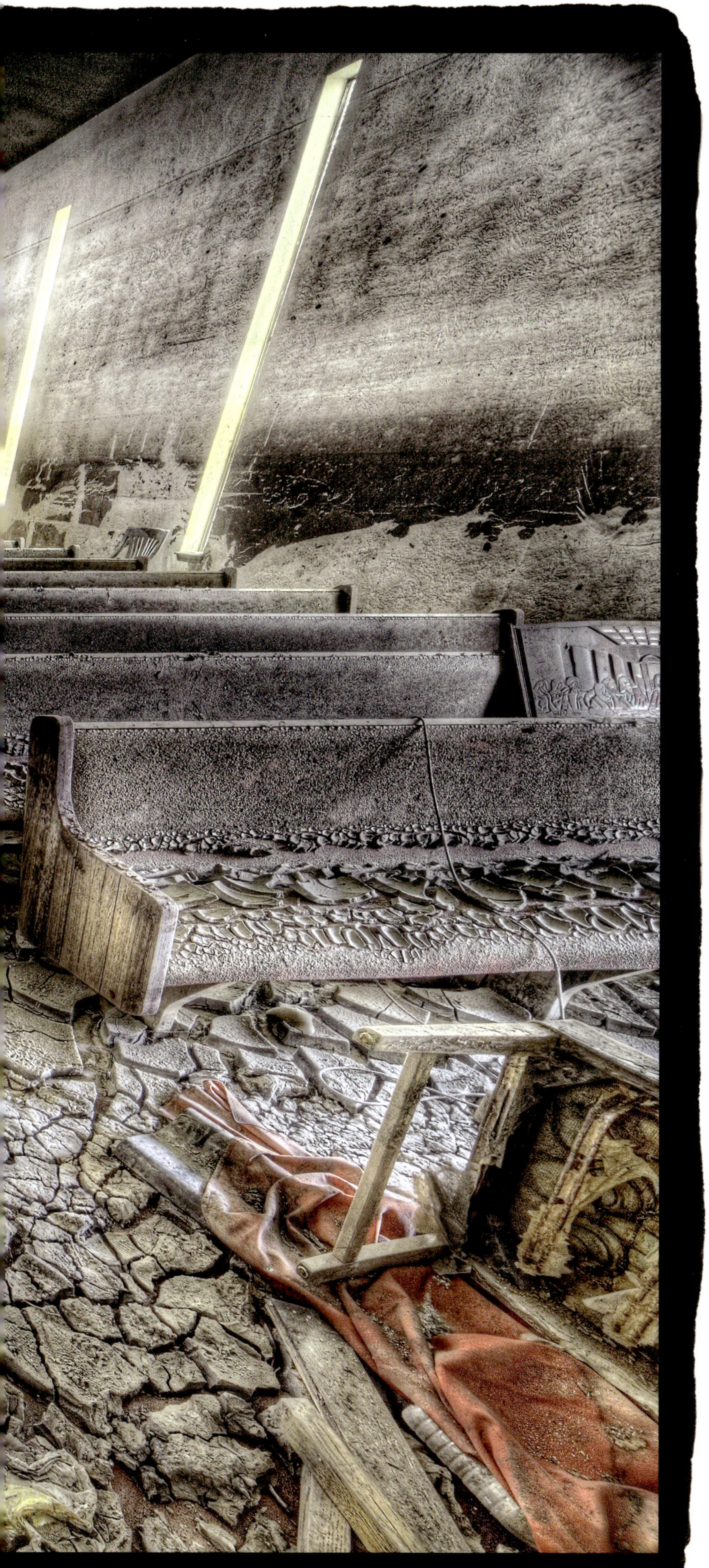

Plant on Church Floor

Church Exit Sign

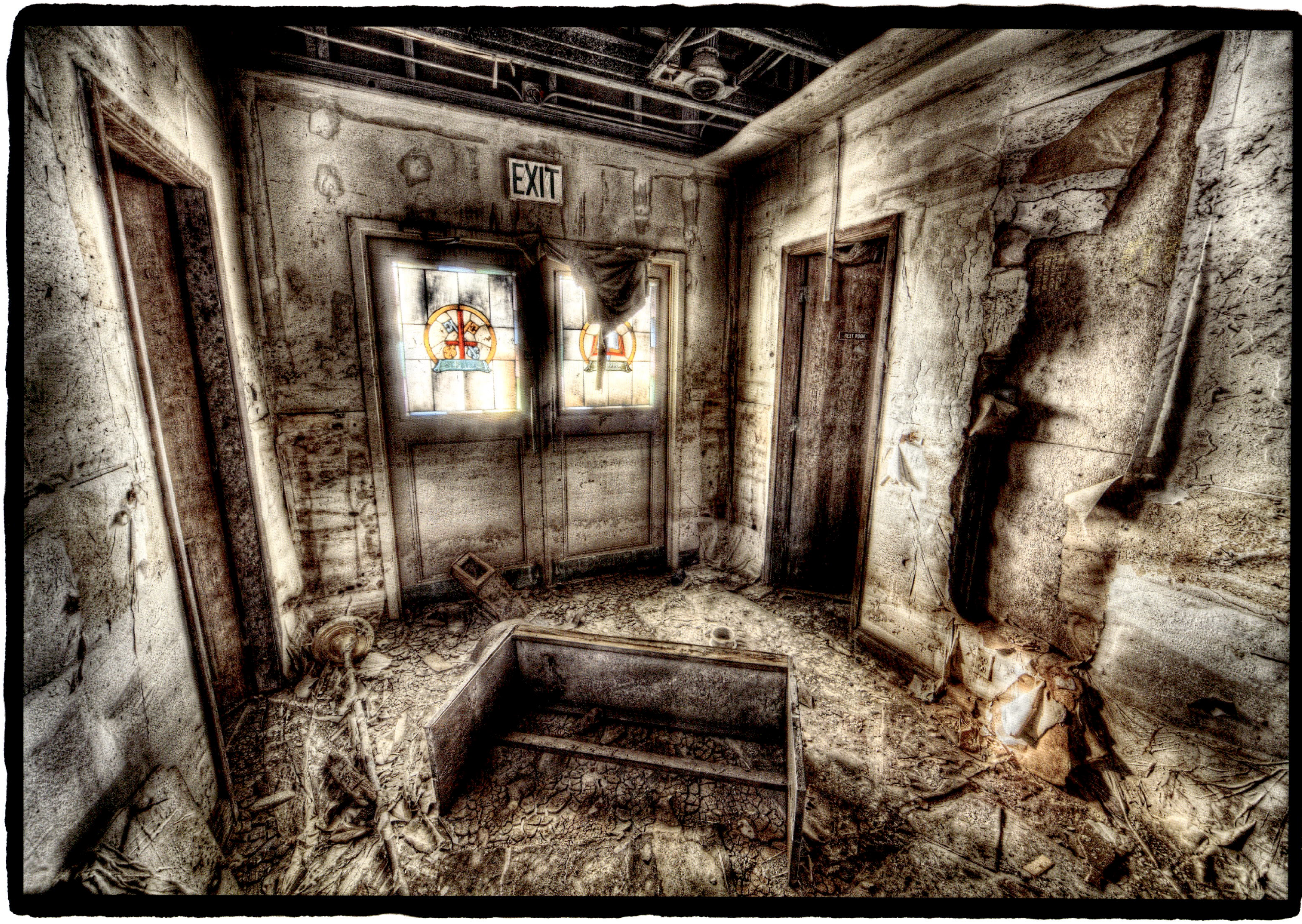
EXIT

Shoe and Gym Bag in Mud

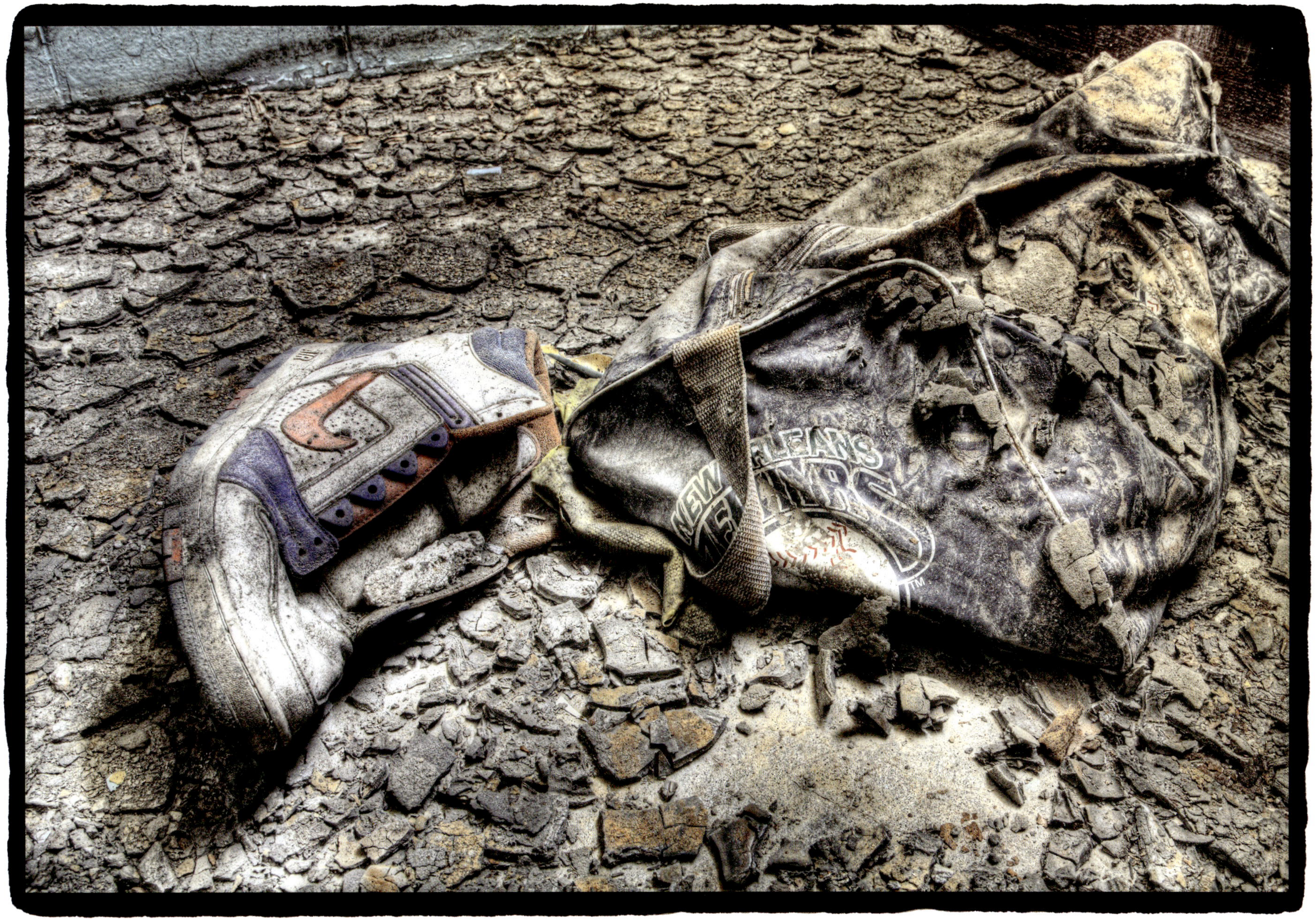
NEW

Helmet and Lockers

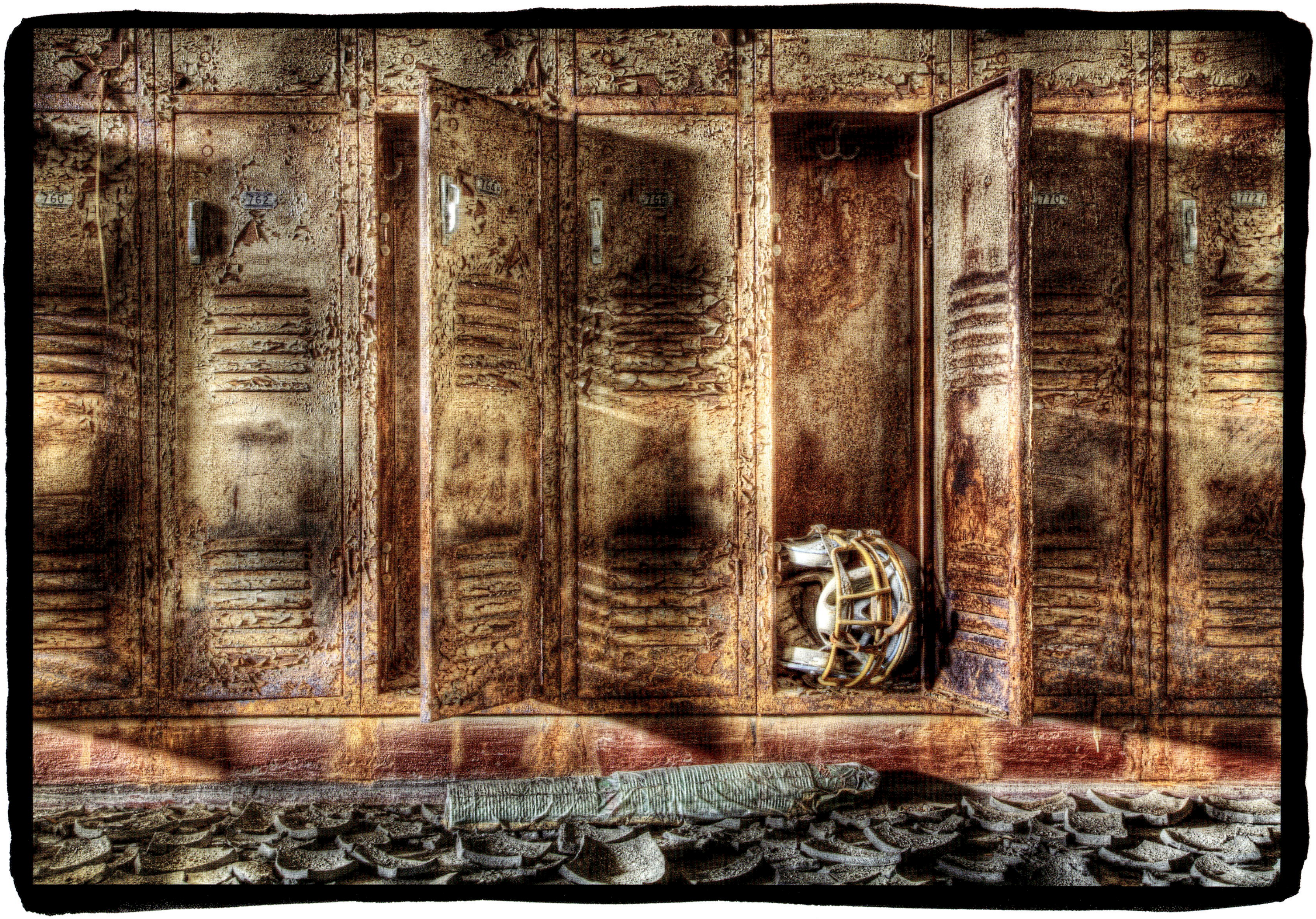
760
762
770
772

Water Fountain in Locker Room

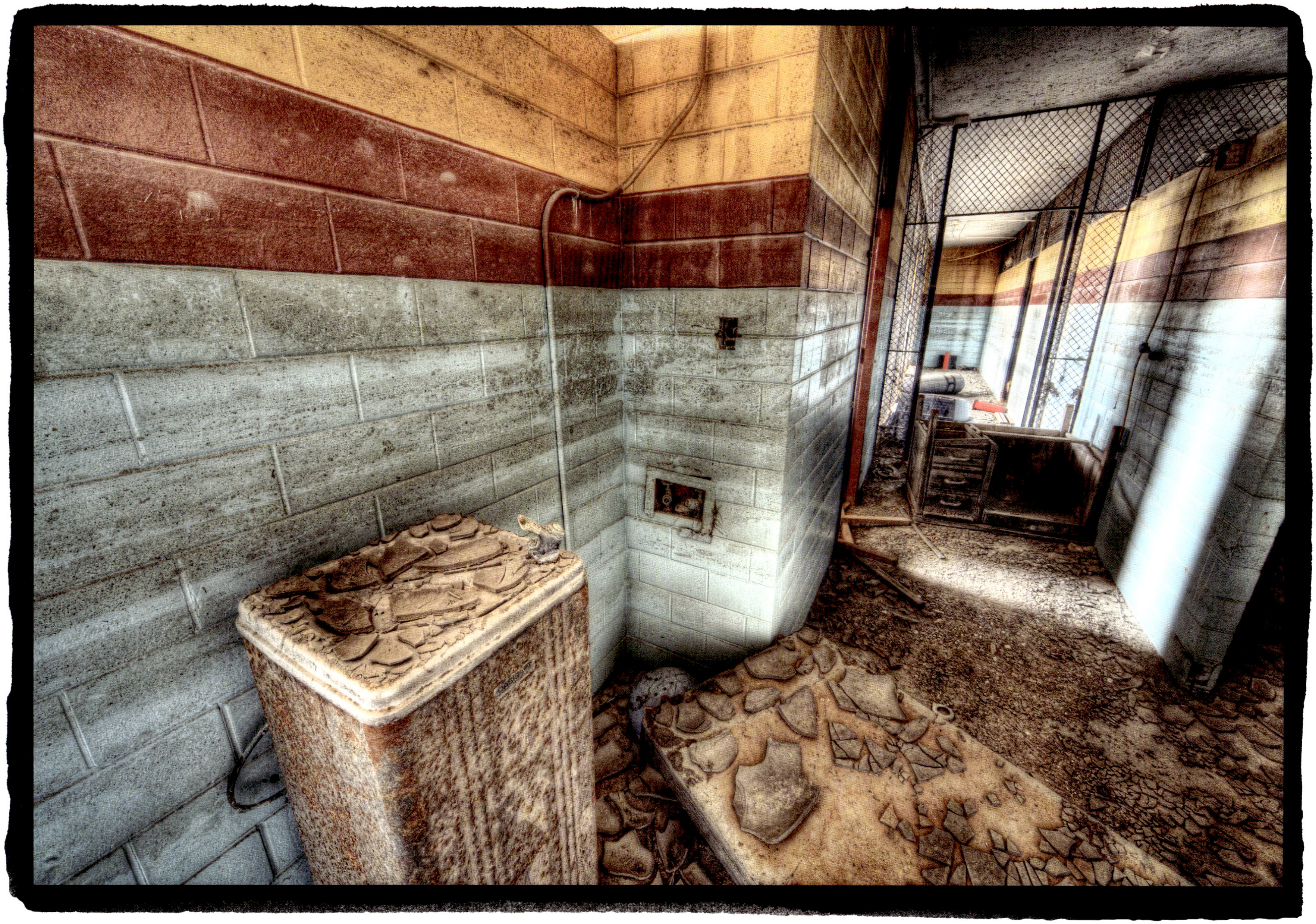

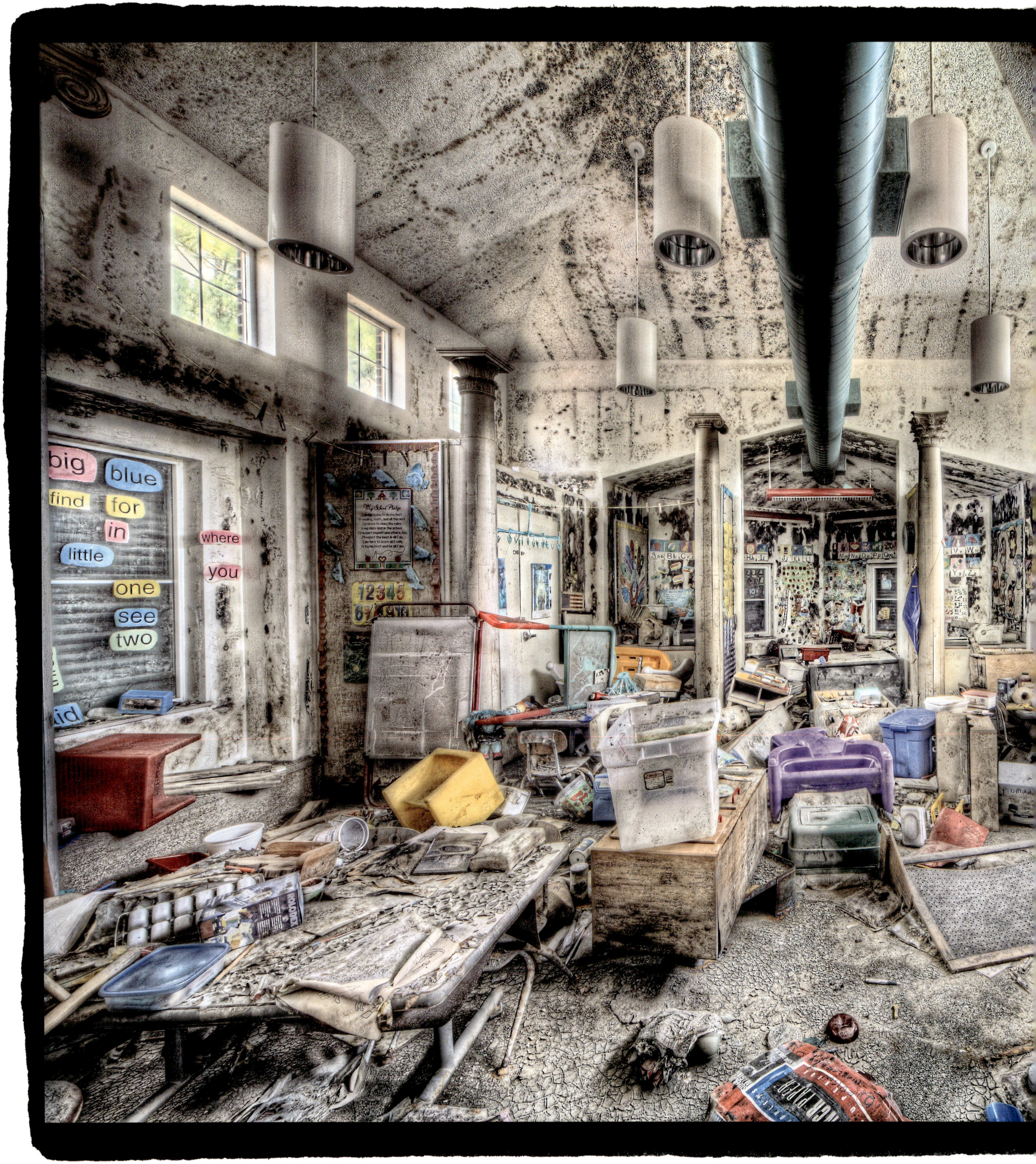
big
blue
find
for
in
little
where
you
one
see
two

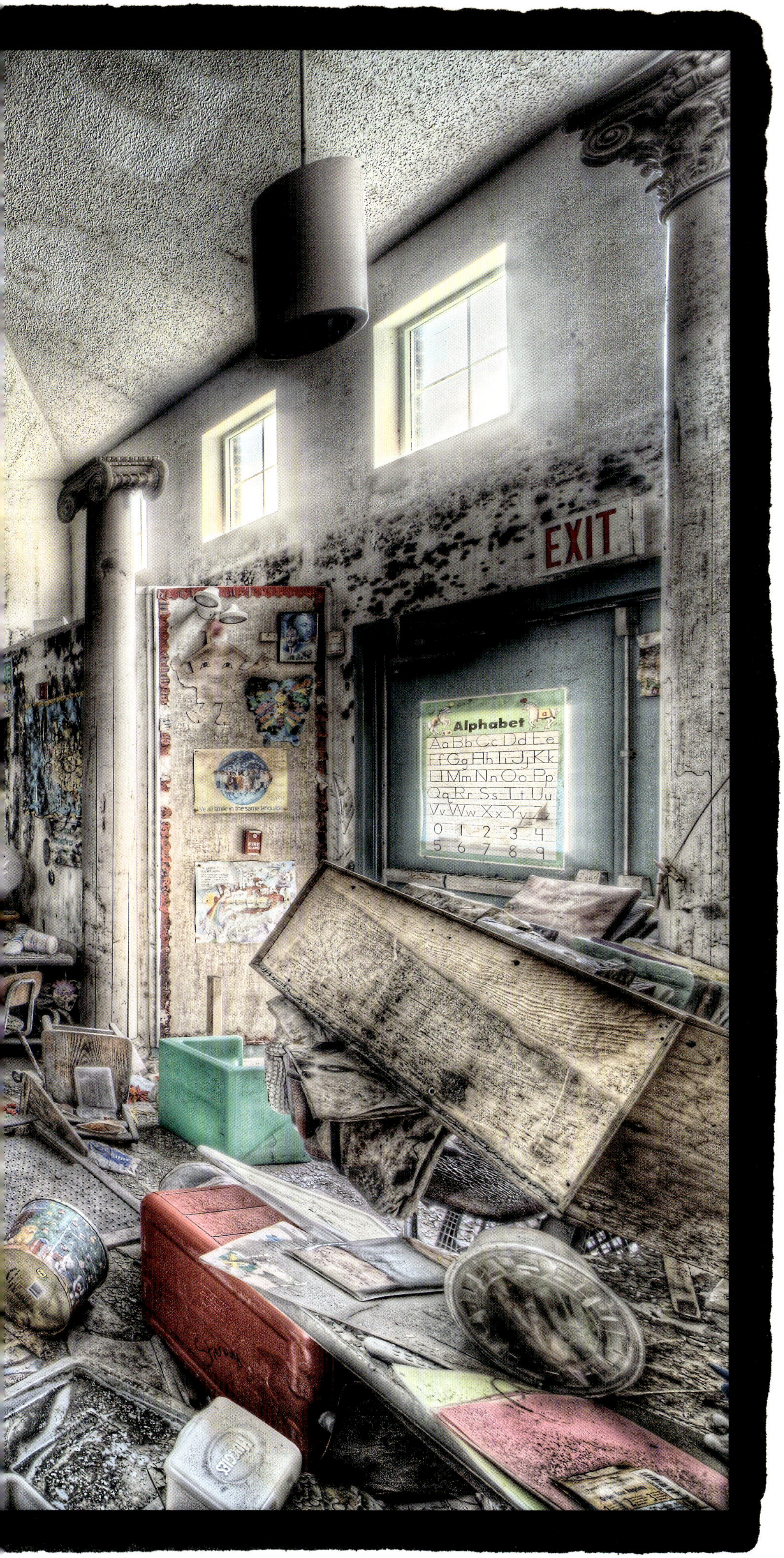

Kindergarten Classroom

Elementary School Mural

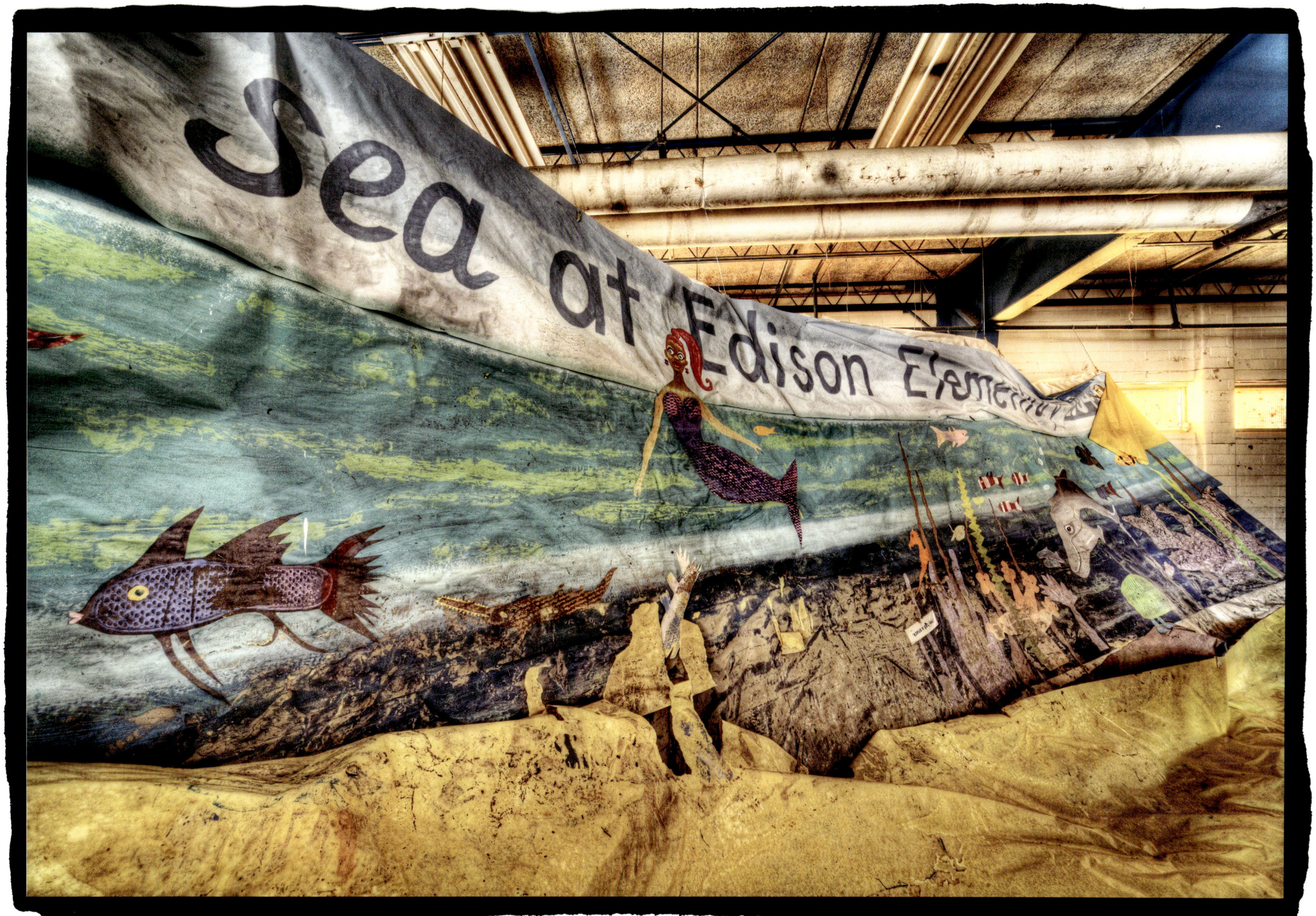
Sea at Edison

School Heating Plant

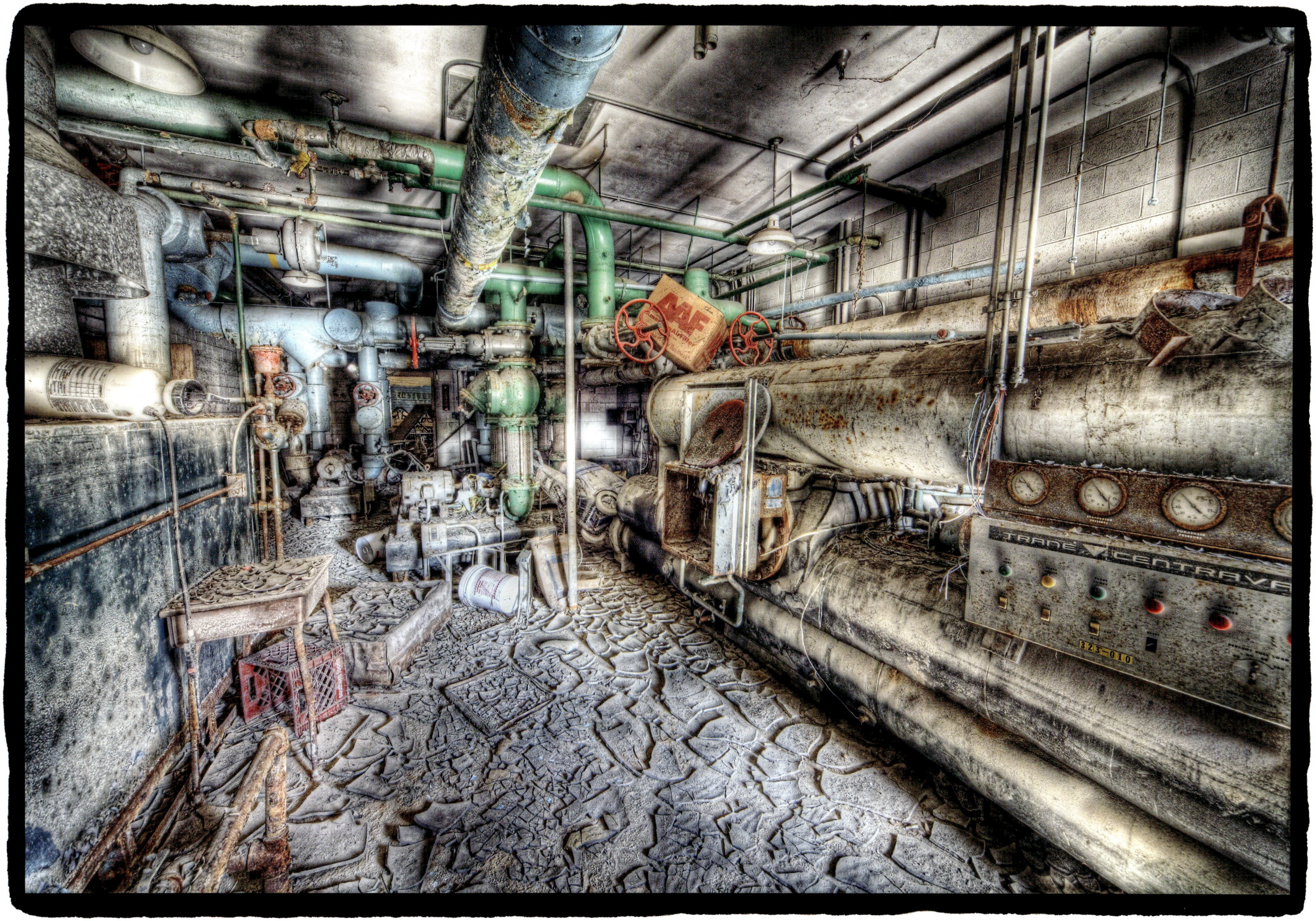
AAF
TRANE

High School Auditorium

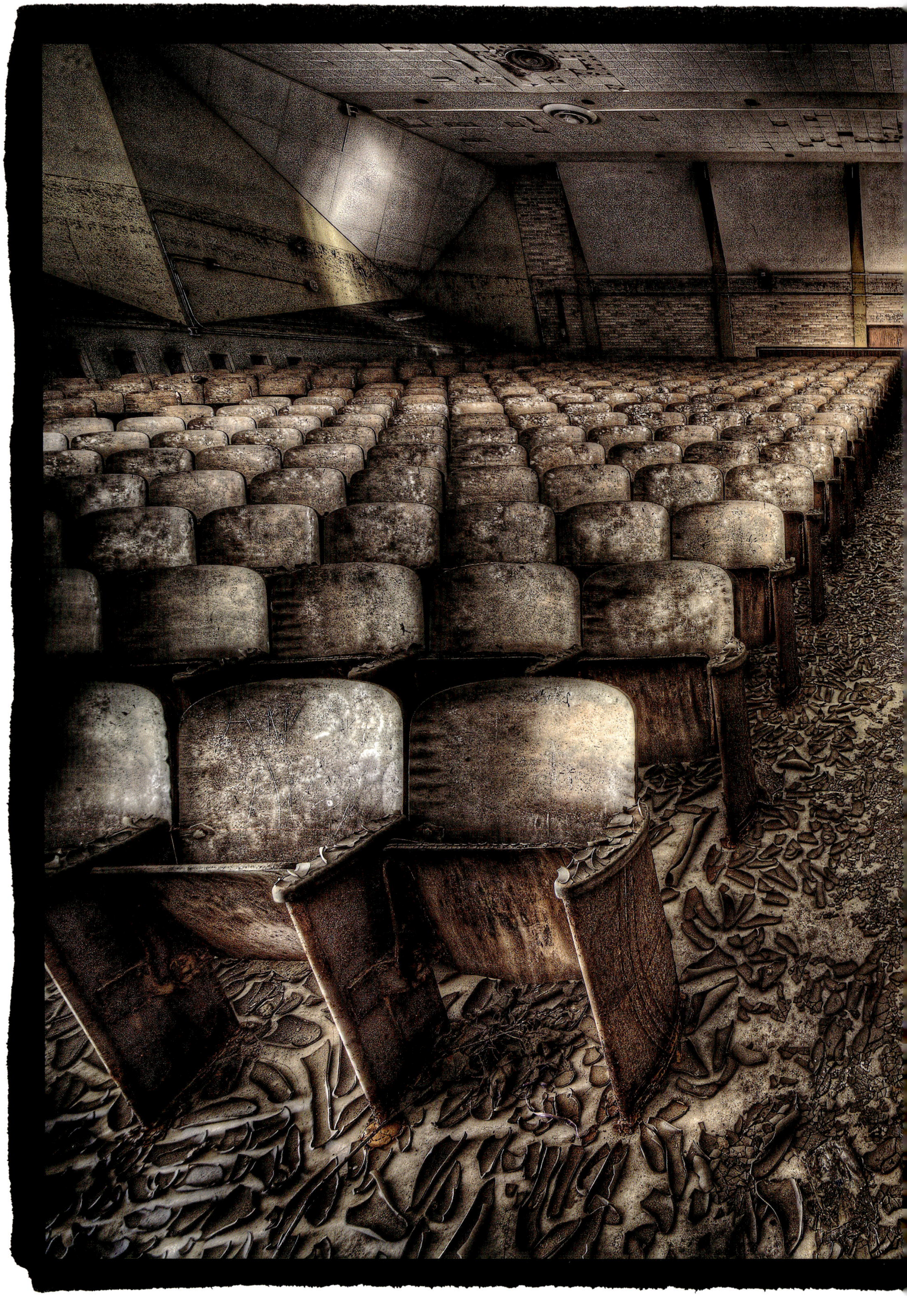

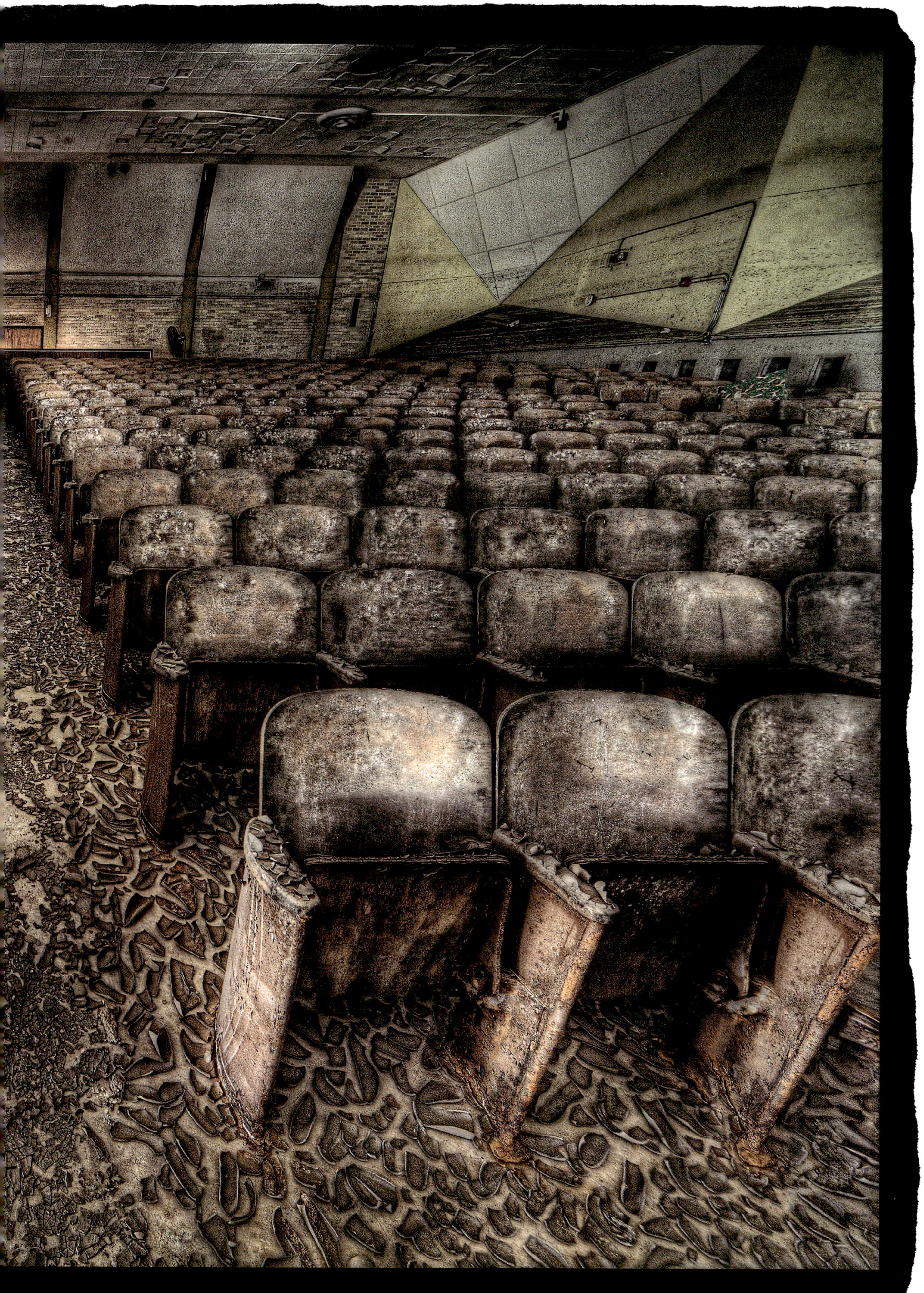

Flowers in Hair Salon

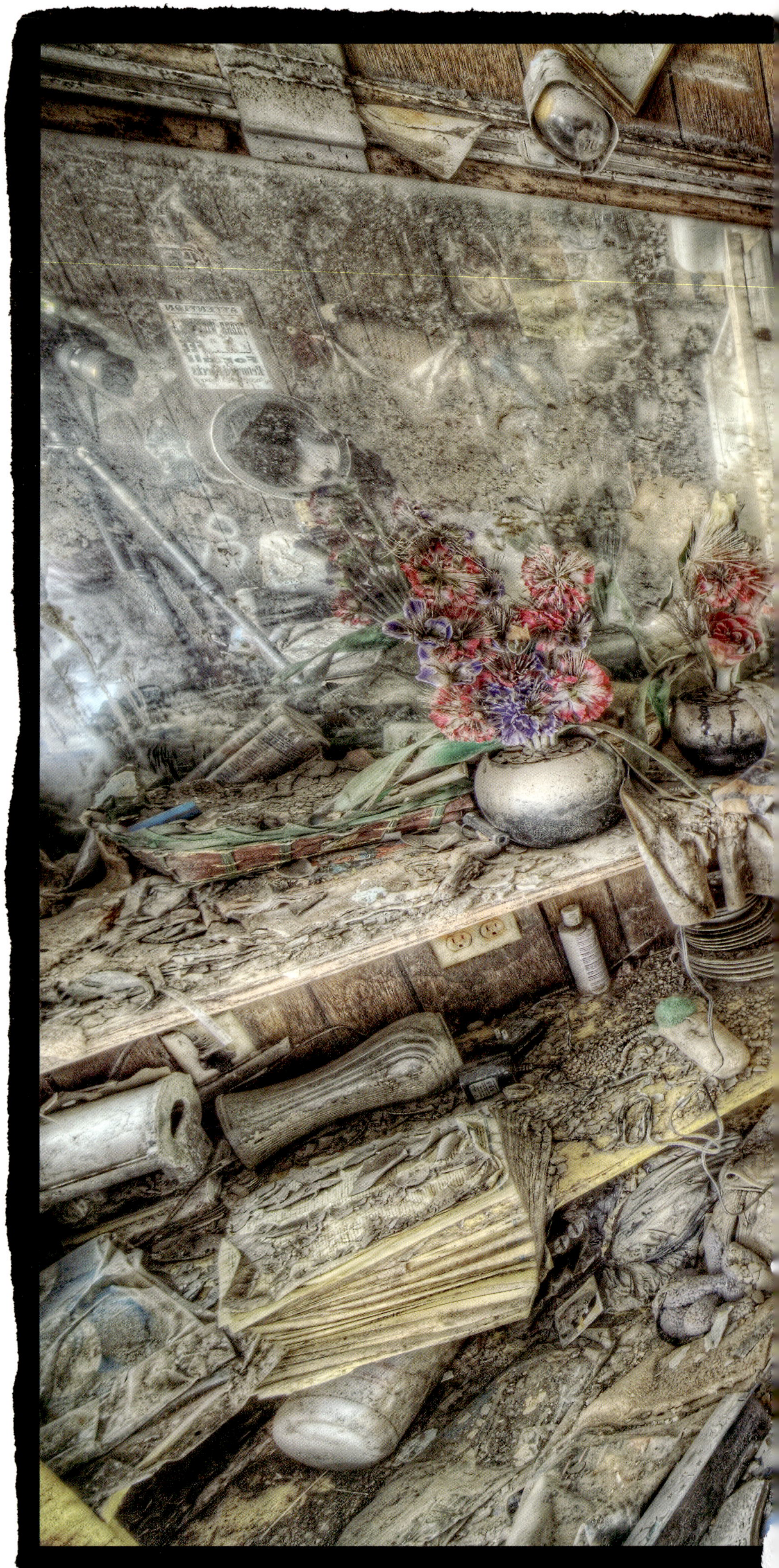

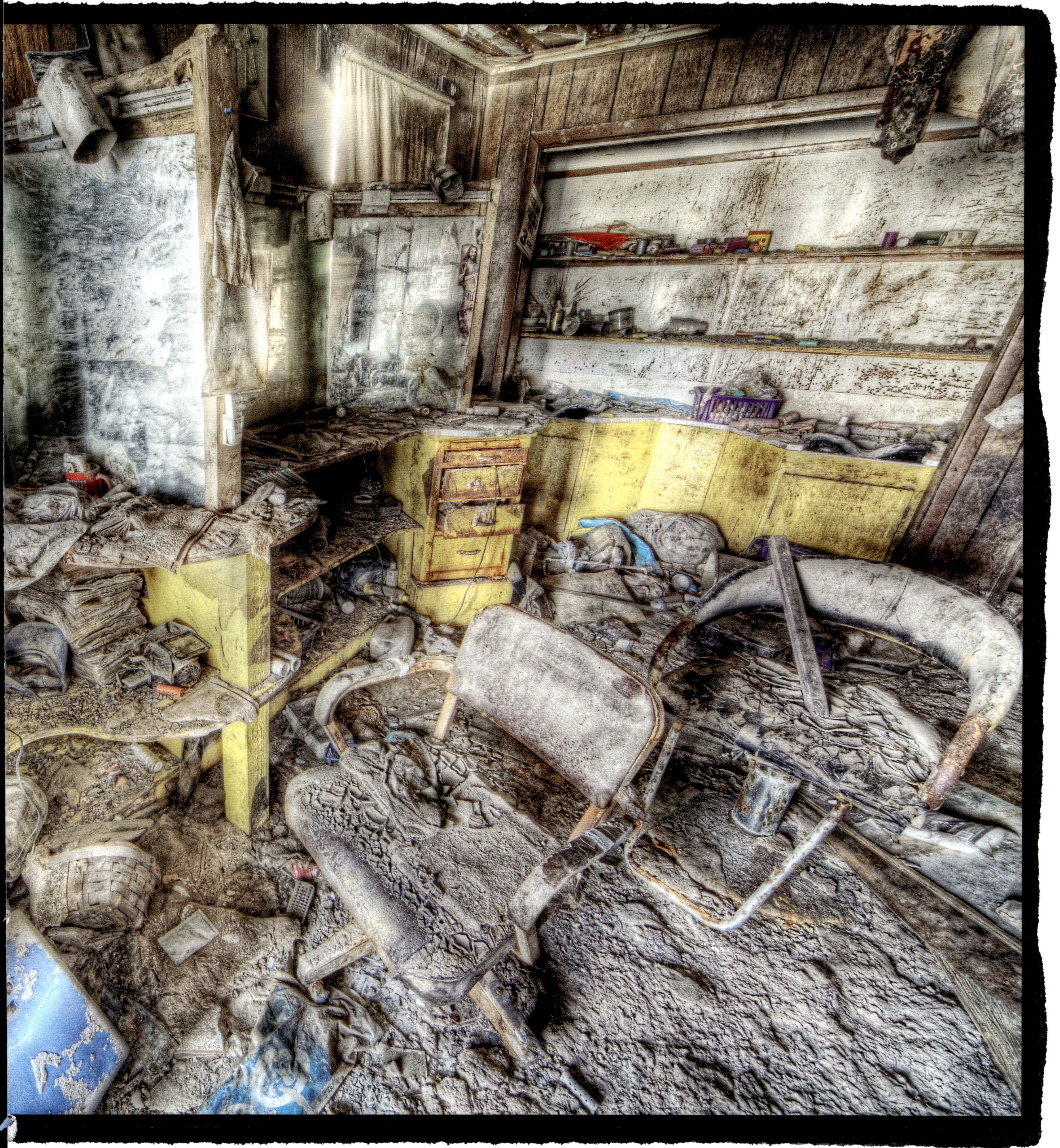

Funeral Parlor Fireplace

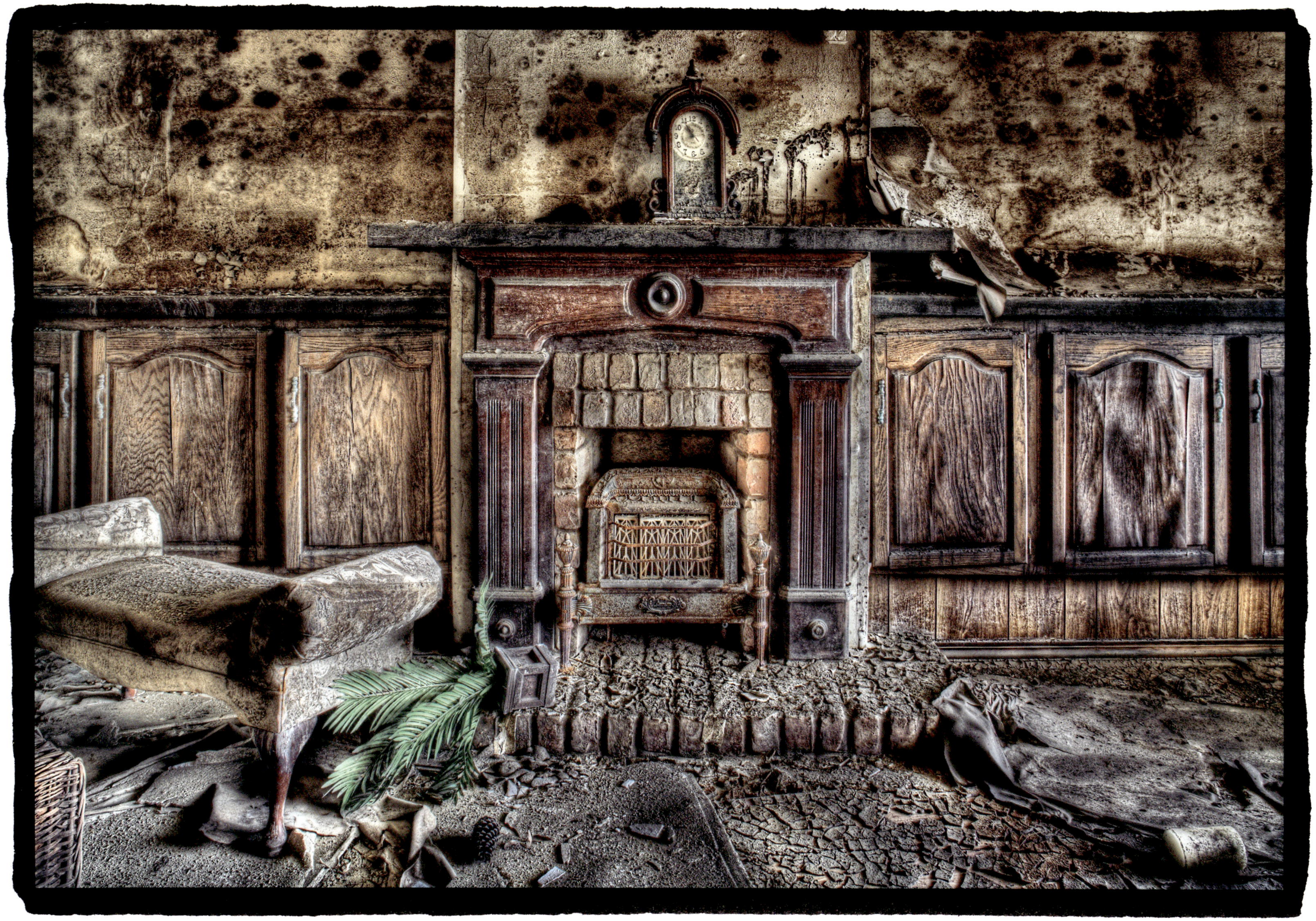

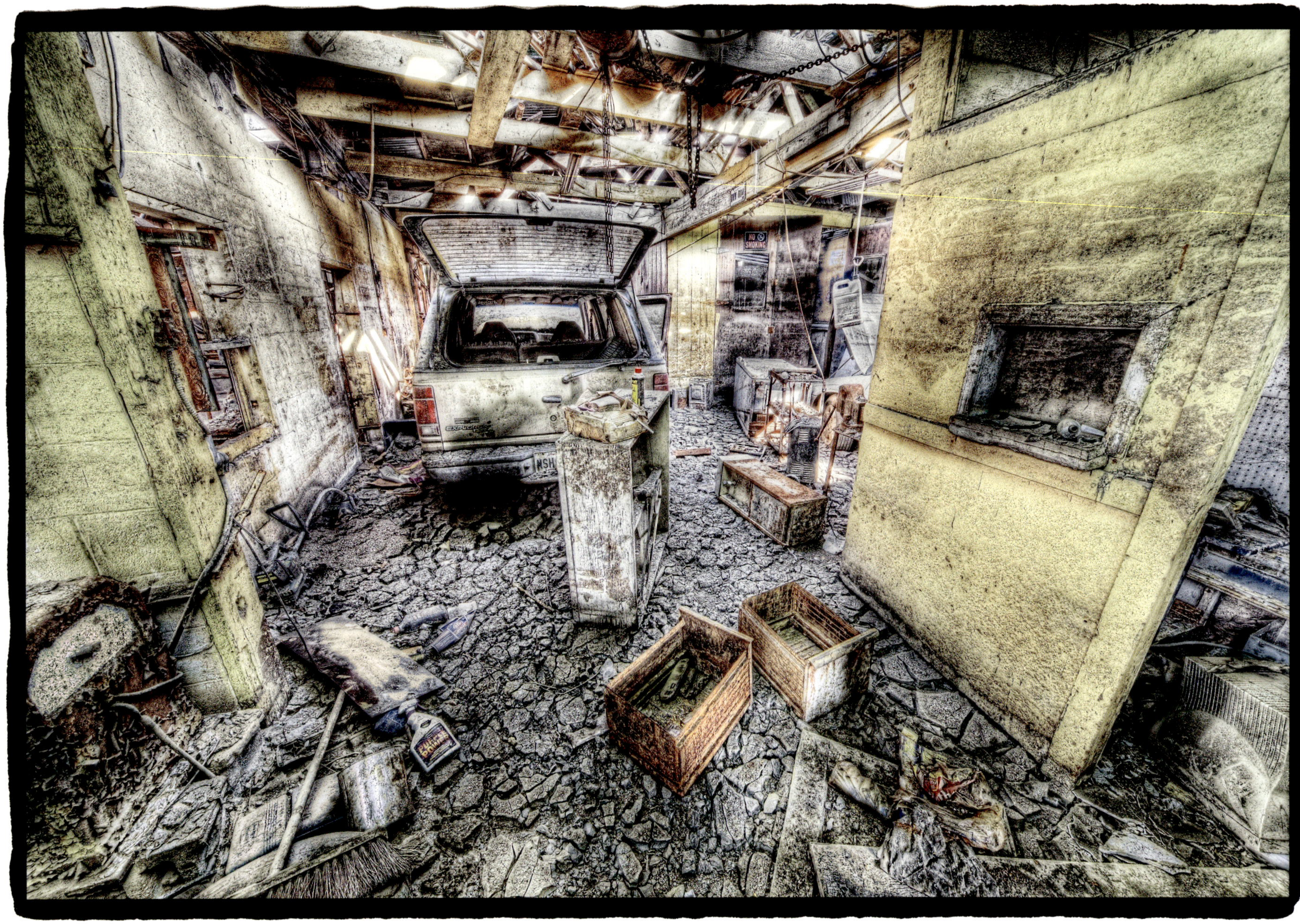

Car in Repair Shop

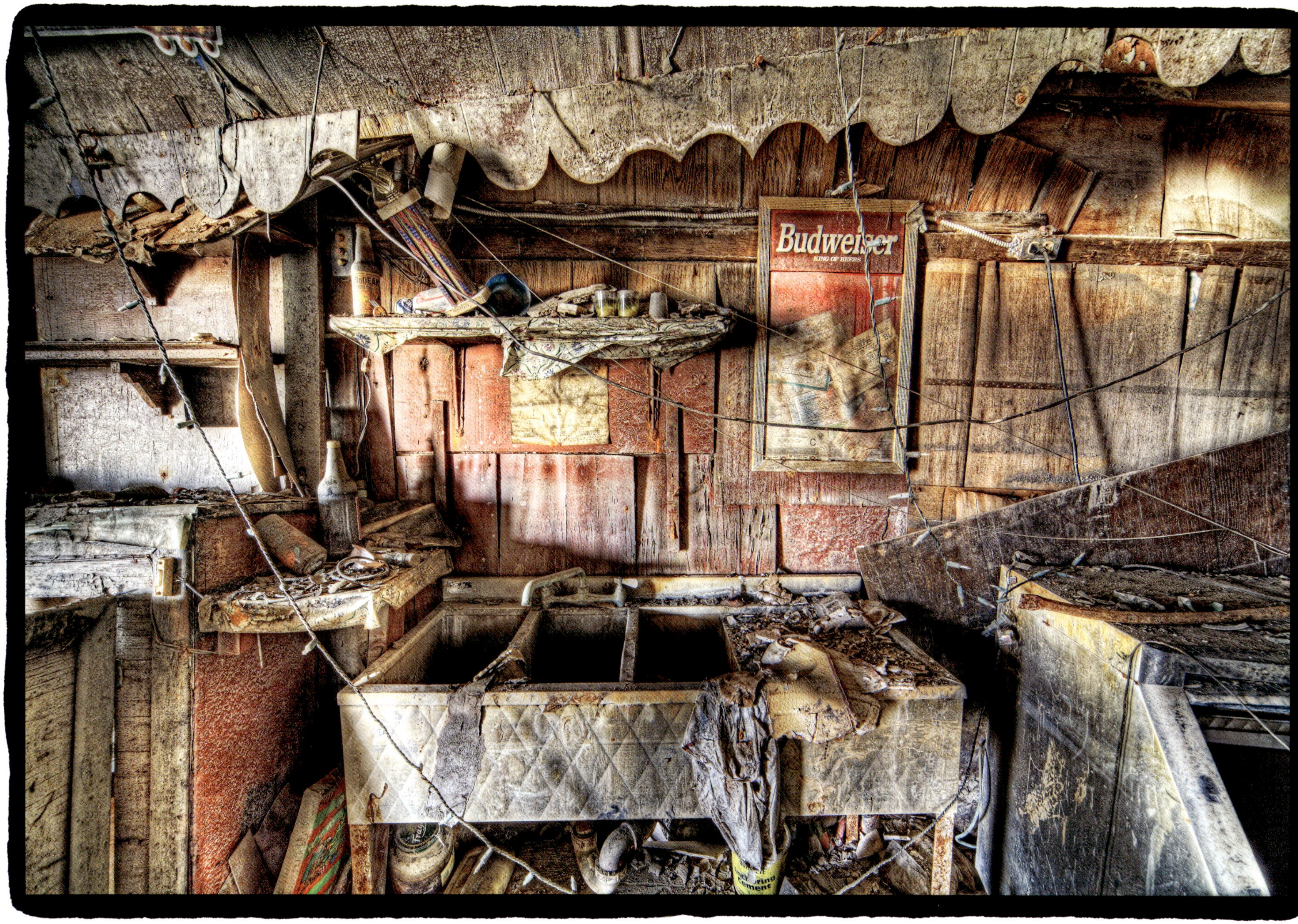

Tavern Sink

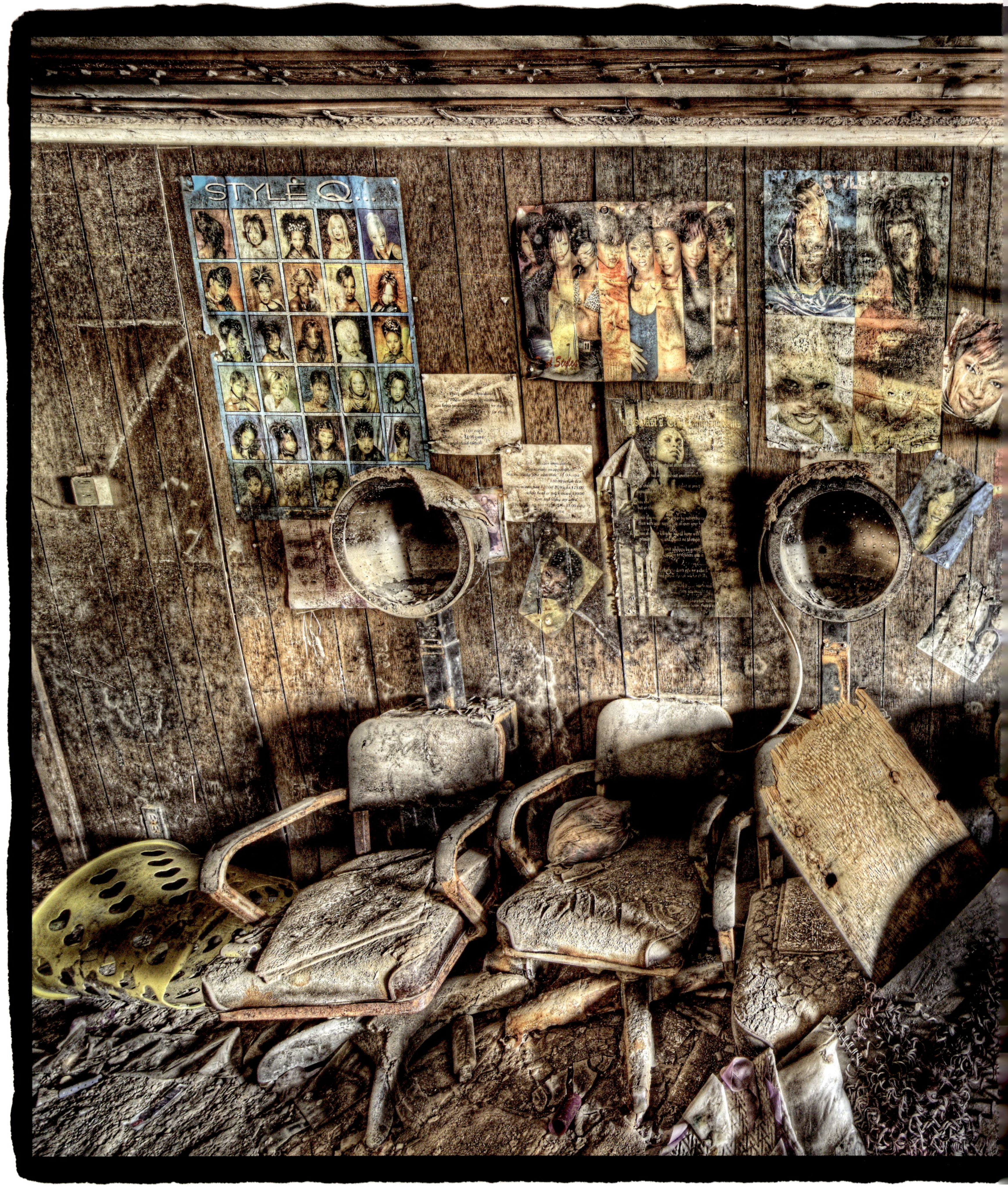
STYLE Q

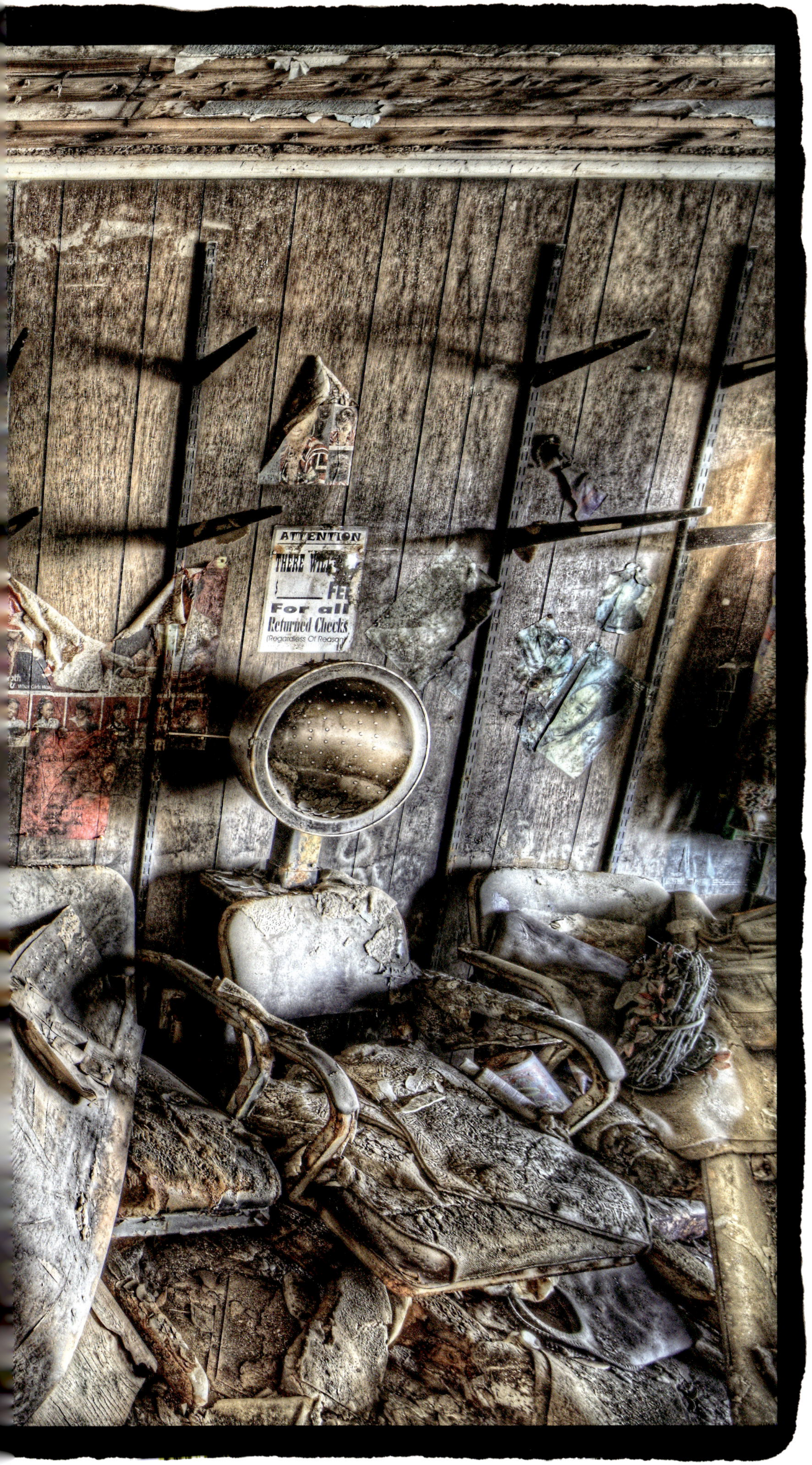

Hair Salon

Hymnal on Pew

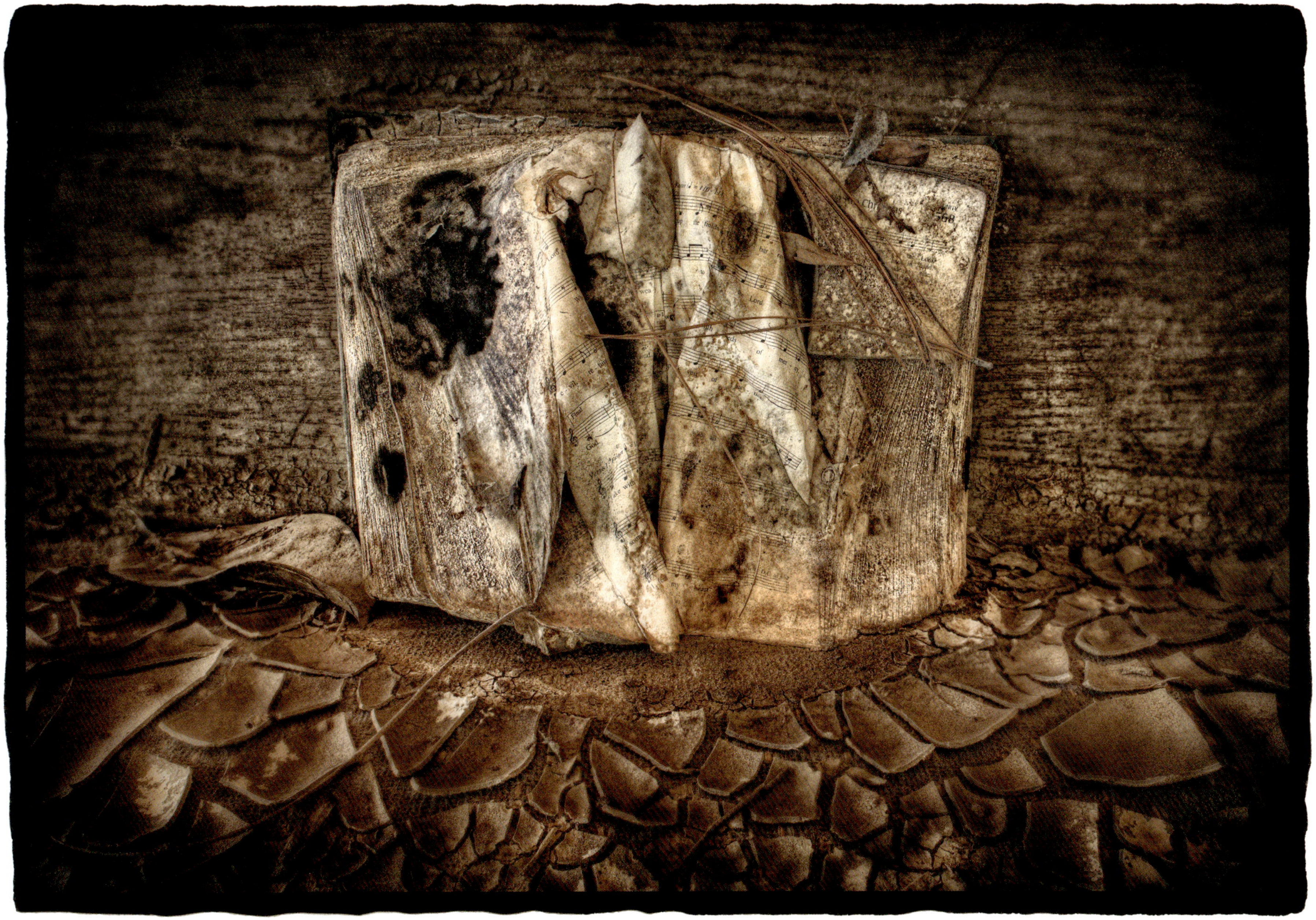

Acknowledgments

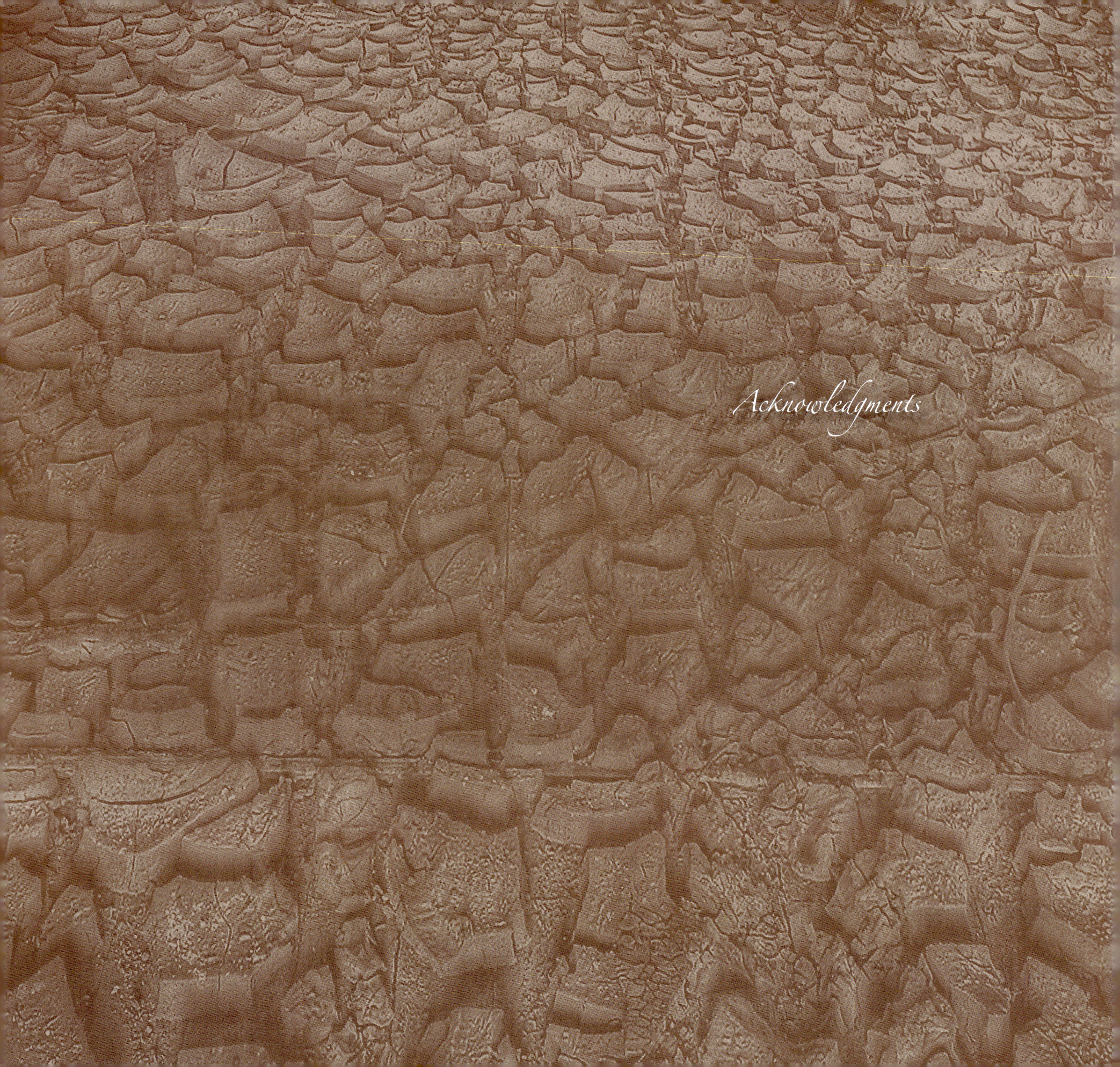

Every photo project has a foundation of friends and colleagues who kindly give time, energy, and guidance to help make it possible and successful. I owe a load of thanks to the following:

Roy Flukinger, who saw the first prints from this series and provided encouragement and enthusiasm, as only an expert in the field could.

O. Rufus Lovett and Frances Lau Lovett, best friends and best humans, who spread the word and made this book gestate.

Arthur Okazaki and Rick Lineberger (Tulane University), who not only welcomed Jill and me to their city but also paved the way with seasoned advice and council.

Vanessa S. Brown and Jeff Louviere, New Orleans artists who became friends. Thanks for that last-minute shower on our way to the airport.

Catherine Steinmann, whose unending energy and support spurred me on no matter how hot or humid the weather.

Golden G. Richard III and Daryl Pfeif-Richard, New Orleans residents who, in the midst of the nightmare of losing their home, showed grace and hospitality—a real class act.

Sherry and Mike Powell, heroes who saved the day when camera gear failed.

Kevin McCaffrey, who opened doors—literally—to his family's loss, trusting strangers to tell the story of tragedy.

Jerry Townsend, who helped tirelessly when help was needed—the true test of friendship.

Mary Lou and Don Wilson—sisters and brothers-in-law don't have to be this big-hearted, but these two make it look easy.

And of course, even if I didn't want to continue living in a happy household, I owe the biggest thanks to my wife, Jill Skupin Burkholder, whose friendship and critical eye combine to make her the ideal companion, both by my side in New Orleans and in life.